Eight Pieces of Silk
What I Could not Tell my Children

Alex Zelczer

Eight Pieces of Silk

What I Could not Tell my Children

In everlasting memory of
my dear Parents, Grandparents, Sisters, Brothers,
Aunts, Uncles, Cousins,
and
the six million innocent Jewish victims
of the most barbarous Nazi persecution
this earth has ever known.

Dedicated to
my children, grandchildren
and great-grandchildren,
whom I so dearly love.

CONTENTS

Introduction *9*

Preface *11*

1. Family, Home and Jewish
   Communal Life *15*
   Parents, Yekusiel Yehuda and Leeba Málka Zelczer /
   Leather business / Surprise arrival in Ungvár: Me! /
   Timely advice / Zelczer bakery / Trips with Father /
   Mechanical interests / Buildings on the spacious property /
   Hidden treasures in the attic / Recreation and Sukkah preparations /
   Outdoor plumbing / Multilingual and multifaceted lives /
   Parents' education and training / Preparing for Sabbath /
   Years in Chéder and Yeshiva /
   Long, rich school days: Hungarian, Hebrew & Yiddish /
   Public schools in Vásárosnamény / Kosher tavern /
   Kehilla life: The Jewish Community of Vásárosnamén /
   Our Rabbi: Eliyahu Kohn / Mátza baking for the Kehilla /
   Private chéder teachers / Vásárosnamény Yeshiva /
   Express Friday-night Bar Mitzvah preparation

2. Life Changes in the
   Shadow of World War II *62*
   Emperor Franz Joseph and the Habsburg Empire /
   Hungarian Communists: My family was left with nothing /
   Children flee in face of war / Growing anti-Semitism all around us /
   Levente Szolgálat: Paramilitary training at age 12 /
   Ostrich politics and psychological denial / Károly Szécsi,
   our "Righteous Gentile" / German soldiers arrive /
   Expulsion orders announced on street corners / Eight pieces of silk:
   The Gray Silk Shawl / Life in the brick factory Ghetto /
   Run? Stay? Agonizing life decisions / Their deception worked /
   Hungarian cattle boxcars to Auschwitz-Birkenau /
   Peepholes in the cattle boxcars / Darkest days on the calendar

3. Auschwitz-Birkenau *97*
   Arrival… / Family are separated / Zehl Appell: Daily physical and
   mental abuse / A day in the Jaworzno Concentration Camp /

Emotional support: Hersh Baer Schwartz / Building a German electric generating plant / Slave-working in concrete for I.G. Farben / Kapo Schteig: Angel of life / Rabbi Friedman of Ráchev / Purchasing Tefillin in Jaworzno? / Talmudic thoughts in Jaworzno / Wretched daily life / Enduring Jaworzno / Gray Silk Shawl "Kamiah" disappears / Hiding from reality — Living on Hope / Perilous Silesian coalmines / "Luxury" store in Jaworzno / A Special Day: An SS bayonet pierces my chest / Surprise: Salvation in the infirmary / Liberation: The brave and victorious Russian soldiers / Caught wearing Wehrmacht Army uniforms

4. After the War   *154*

Return to Vásárosnamény — by foot / Safe House in Krakow: Jews in a danger-zone again!! / Delicious cheese noodles served in carved table holes / Russian Jewish Captain in Stáry Sácz / Father's cousin, Dezsõ Zelcer / Károly Szécsy revisited: Invitation to a family feast / Sign of life from my sister in Bergen-Belsen / Complex decisions in Vásárosnamény / Indebted to the Russians and Americans / Last Three Straws; Russian Communists / The departure / Munkatábor Slaves / Brother's escape / Four categories of Concentration Camps / Dire need for DP Camps / Survivors' needs in DP Camps / How Russia dealt with Nazis / How the US and Great Britain dealt with Nazis / The Ernie Pyle / Bellefaire: The first step towards rebuilding life / Life and Liberty: The treasured freedoms of America

5. My Reflections   *203*

Christian anti-Semitism / Introduction to hatred / Jews hiding among Christians / Jewish parents' dilemma / Ghettos compared: Original ghettos and later ghettos / Denial and desperate hope / Promotion — Profit — Prestige / The long and precarious exile / Relentless pursuit / Youthful recollections / Sarcastic note to the International Red Cross / How does one kill a God?

Rational thoughts: A survivor's observations, insights, & lessons   *225*

Holocaust timeline: As experienced by a survivor from Hungary   *231*

WWII timetable and notes   *237*

Acknowledgements   *240*

Introduction

I am a survivor of the Jewish Holocaust of 1939-1945. I was brutally dispatched in cattle boxcar trains with my parents and five of my eight siblings from the Ghetto of Beregszász, Hungary, to the Auschwitz-Birkenau concentration camp complex. This occurred shortly after our family turned down a friendly Gentile's offer to take shelter in his farm.

Within hours of arrival in Auschwitz-Birkenau, I was cut off and separated from my parents and siblings. At age sixteen and a half, I found myself all alone in a wild and strange inhuman wasteland.

After a few weeks of daily torment in Auschwitz-Birkenau, the German SS drove me to the Jaworzno Concentration Camp where I slave-worked in the concrete construction division of the I.G. Farben Company, building a new electric power station for *Oberschlesien* (Upper Silesia). Later on that autumn, I worked long shifts in the perilous Carlsgrube and Fredrichsgrube coal mines.

After liberation by the Russian Army in late January of 1945, I quickly made my torturous way home — needlessly, as it turned out, for no parents or siblings were there waiting for me. Subsequently, during the next seven months, four withered siblings found their way home from various liberated German concentration camps. Sadly, four other siblings and both parents never returned.

Within a few months, we refurbished our parents' gutted house and bakery and ventured to reopen the Zelczer Family Bakery business. Before long, disheartened with the local situation, we clandestinely disappeared into the night. Several weeks later, we found ourselves in the crowded DP camps of

U.S. occupied Western Germany.

In 1947 I came to America, where I married, raised a family, and worked as a baker, electrician, and ultimately, as an electrical contractor and businessman.

This book is a detailed report of my life experiences from the time I was a young boy living with parents and 9 siblings in Vásárosnamény, Hungary, and through our engulfment in a deluge of Nazi propaganda and hatred, murderous anti-Semitism, and the daily horrors of Hitler's "Final Solution."

In this document, I share my intimate feelings of hope, alarm, terror and despair throughout this time. I recount the pain of separation from my beloved family, and provide a full description of the difficult conditions I endured as a teenager, incarcerated in the death camps of Auschwitz-Birkenau, and later in the Jaworzno "work-to-death" Concentration Camp.

I describe my liberation in 1945 at the hands of Russian forces and my subsequent efforts to find surviving family members. The book includes a detailed description of daily life in the DP camps of Germany and, finally, my arrival in the United States of America. I also include references and physical, statistical and political information relating to the periods leading up to, and after World War II Europe.

More than just a personal history, this story is also that of numerous others who did not survive to tell theirs.

Therefore, I herewith transmit my experiences to the younger generations of the world. I emphasize that I feel obliged to tell the history for the sake of the memory of my dear parents, grandparents, siblings, aunts, uncles, cousins, neighbors and distant relatives, of blessed memory — all of whom were among the six million innocent Jews murdered by the German, Hungarian, Ukrainian, Polish, Slovak, Romanian, Yugoslavian Nazis and their enthusiastic accomplices.

Since the collective voices of my extended family and friends were silenced forever, I must speak for them now.
No one else can — or ever will.

Preface

During World War I and up to the political upheaval of 1938/1939, Jewish men in Europe served bravely and honorably in the Hungarian, Czechoslovakian, Polish, Romanian and other national armed forces. Many of my family served valiantly, and indeed, several died and a number were severely wounded in these various armies. In fact, for hundreds of years, we had been law-abiding, taxpaying and productive citizens of these countries.

Our ancestors were active in commerce, the arts and many trades. They created businesses, large and small, which employed many thousands. They founded industries and were involved in small- and large-scale farming, all in the framework of exemplary and first-rate citizenship.

And yet, all of the above notwithstanding, my family, as most Jews of Europe, were one day sadistically collected, jammed at gunpoint into railroad cattle boxcars and shipped off to be destroyed in clandestine murder camps.

As a mid-teenager, I found myself ruthlessly catapulted by the rapid and sweeping developments in the worldwide historical events of World War II. My young life was propelled from a nearly placid rural existence into the burning blaze of a mad and newly conceived partnership of the German and Hungarian devils.

The German-Hungarian annihilation plans were clear: to work to death; to shoot on sight; to drown in raging rivers; to freeze on desolate roads; to choke with gas; and to cremate all peoples they determined to be their enemies, or simply useless in their eyes. The choice of murder methods was up to the Germans and their eager cohorts.

After my liberation from captivity in the concentration camps, these horrible memories and my family's near-annihilation were impossible to avoid. In order to go on with my day-to-day or hour-to-hour life, I had to wage a fight for my survival over and over again. This battle took place within my anxious, frightened mind. I needed to escape the searing, painful and vivid memories of the unspeakable terror and waves of fanatical hate which I had experienced in Europe. I searched for a way to stop the tormenting nightmares and regain a life of sanity and normalcy. My need to accommodate a new and personal life became an overriding purpose.

From the time World War II ended in May of 1945, I deliberately secluded the recollections of Beregszász, Auschwitz-Birkenau and Jaworzno in a hidden corner of the labyrinth of my brain. They were much too agonizing and excruciating to deal with. I became a full-time fugitive from the short but hefty part of my brief history that contained the massive madness of militant intolerance and bigotry, which had enmeshed me and my family during my youthful and formative years.

I was mentally unable to find release — unable to tell my children even a coherent snippet of my Holocaust experiences, or recall those who disappeared from my hometown Vásárosnamény, without choking on names of murdered families. These memories were scorching, and caused nightmares which only renewed the terrible suffering.

My young children astutely sensed my mental throbbing, and soon stopped inquiring about the numbered tattoo — A.9561 — on my arm or about their never-to-be-seen grandparents, aunts, uncles, cousins and other relatives they longed to meet.

I had to find a way to live as normal and peaceful a life as possible. I looked for a means to deal with the deep mental intrusions of my ordeal and tame them, so as to avoid the searing pain and the repetitious frightful nightmares of murder and carnage fueled by inhuman hate and envy.

I found a solution in the form of a mind-game. I took an imaginary trip down to the basement where I dug a bottomless make-believe hole, into which I dumped all my past troubles. I then covered it up with dirt, stomped on it with both feet, and finally pulled a large heavy rug over it. I mentally buried all the painful memories!

As long as there was nothing to reawaken them, my nightmares and heartbreaking sensations decreased, both in number and intensity. This tactic worked relatively well, though it had to be repeated periodically.

Five decades since the Holocaust passed quickly. At the beginning of the sixth decade, at the urging of my friend, Dr. Leatrice Rabinsky, an internationally-known Holocaust educator and authority, I began to invest a great deal of thought into articulating my history.

Toward that end, I became one of a group of survivor-lecturers at the Face to Face Holocaust Education Program at Congregation Shaarey Tikvah in a suburb of Cleveland, Ohio. Face to Face is an educational effort in which more than 2,300 middle and high school students participate each year. On occasion, I lecture in other frameworks as well.

While giving these presentations I sensed that the knowledge of these horrifying facts was sorely lacking. As a result, I firmly concluded that as disconcerting as my chronicle may be, I must tell it as I lived it — beginning to end. I now feel consciously obligated to inform the world and keep alive the memory of the Holocaust, along with its effect on my family, my hometown and the Jewish people.

Now, at my advanced age, I am inspired to tell you this

story. It is my fervent wish that this teaching will continue after I am gone.

While the majority of the European population either actively persecuted or simply turned their backs on us, a number of warm-hearted and courageous Gentiles did indeed help, taking extremely serious risks upon themselves and their families to save Jews and politically endangered Christians. We must be forever indebted to these *"Righteous Among the Nations"* and be grateful for their courageous and compassionate human conduct.

We must resolve to educate and inspire our families, our friends, and even our enemies, regarding the importance of freedom, tolerance, fairness, equality, acceptance and dignity for all human beings.

This lesson, also, is one about which I cannot afford to keep silent. The luxury of silence is no longer an option for me. I must tell my story, so others may learn how to avoid a replication of this great tragedy.

To facilitate a clear understanding of this difficult subject, I wrote this book as follows: The story begins with a discussion of my family and life in Hungary before the onset of this horrific period. It continues with a personal account of the Nazi period's impact on my life. In the concluding chapters, I discuss my reflections of the war period based on the experiences I felt and endured. [As each essay is an independent story, some repetition can be expected and is important to the flow of the narrative.]

❈ 1 ❈
Family, Home and Jewish Communal Life

Parents: Yekusiel Yehuda and Leeba Malka Zelczer

My father, Yekusiel Yehuda (Salamon) Zelczer, whom we addressed as "Tattee," was the firstborn son of Eliezer and Hinda (neé Kohn) Zelcer. My grandfather spelled his name Zelcer — not Zelczer. Other relatives spelled it in different ways.

My best estimate is that my father was born around 1888/1889 in Kralovsky Chlmec, then part of Czechoslovakia and the Austro-Hungarian Empire. Generally, we used a shorter Hungarian name, Királyhelmec or Helmec.

Depending on the time and political developments, Helmec was under the successive rule of the far-flung Austro-Hungarian Empire, Czechoslovakia, Hungary and Slovakia.

My father's parents, Eliézer and Hinda, owned and operated the Zelcer Bakery in Helmec. The bakery was located on a long main street which cut through the center of town and led to the nearby small town of Perbenyik, about four kilometers away. Perbenyik was on the main railroad line leading to the larger cities of Chap, Kassa, Munkács, Prague, Budapest and Bucharest.

Helmec, like many other cities and towns in the area, had a sizeable Jewish community, and Jews were an important part of its economic life and development. As an indication of Jewish integration into the overall community of Helmec during the World War I era, it is worth noting that of the 148 Jewish families living in Helmec in the year 1914, no less than 67 (45.3%) contributed their members to the Hungarian Armed forces.

My father attended yeshiva in the town of Hegyaljamáda which we often shortened to Máade, just as we did with the long names of countless other cities and towns. At various times, the Yeshiva had from 65 to 90 full-time students. The *Rosh Yeshiva* (Rabbi and Dean) was Rabbi Mordechai Yehuda Leib Winkler. Rabbi Winkler died in 1932 at the age of 88.

Leather business

In 1906, when he was 18, my father left the Yeshiva to learn a business and a trade, as did his close friends. He signed up as an apprentice to his older cousin, Ármin (Aharon) Kohn who had a leather design and shoemaker-supply business in Királyhelmec. During his three or four years of training, Father lived with his own parents who resided nearby.

The training consisted of designing, cutting, and sewing colorful ladies' handbags, leather uppers of ladies' and men's shoes, as well as boots, lumbar supports, hernia belts and sandals. The supply business also sold thick leather soles, heel-protectors, wooden nails, lining, glue and general repair materials to the shoemakers in the area. Quality ready-made shoes were rare in those days.

A condition of his training contract prohibited him from opening a competing business within a certain number of kilometers from his training-master's location. For this reason, when my father finished his training, he opened a leather-goods business in the nearby town of Vásárosnamény where he had a monopoly for some years. He was happy and successful in his business, and due to expansion employed a number of workers. He produced high-quality footwear with unique designs and modern color combinations. The products he manufactured were able to withstand the area's abundance of rain, sticky clay-like mud, snow, ice, and sleet. Custom-designed ladies' handbags were also among his specialties.

Passport picture of my father, circa, 1937, at age 49. Two official passport stamps of Vásárosnamény are visible on both top corners, as is his signature 'Zelczer Salamon' on bottom.*

In 1911, at around age 23, my father married Myrtle Reichfeld of Ungvár (now Uzgorod, Ukraine). Myrtle was the daughter of Yosef Reichfeld, an insurance agent in Ungvár, one of Czechoslovakia's larger cities. Yosef Reichfeld's father, Baruch, (d. 1911), was a *Dayan* (religious judge) in the city, and the son-in-law of Rabbi Chaim Tzvi (Hirsh) Mannheimer, the Chief Rabbi of Ungvár from 1860 until his death in 1886.

In 1913, Myrtle gave birth to a lovely girl named Gittel (Gizi). Unfortunately, Myrtle died as a direct result of this childbirth. My father remarried to my mother Leeba Málka, who lavished Gittel with love and kindness. Gittel thrived and grew up happily with my family in Vásárosnamény. The love and devotion in our home was such that I was not even aware

---

* After our deportation to the Beregszász Ghetto in 1944, our neighbors and/or vandals destroyed all our family pictures. Upon my return to Vásárosnamény in 1945, I found this solitary picture lying in the corner of the compost pile in the back of our yard. Family and friends gave us some additional pre-war pictures presented in this book.

that Gittel was not my full sister. It was only after World War II that my older brother Matyu told me the story of our half-sister Gittel and her mother Myrtle Reichfeld. (Some families did not disclose stepchild information in order to safeguard the orphaned child from teasing by other siblings).

In 1914 my father married my mother, Leeba Málka (neé Laura Frankel) of Ungvár, who was then 17 years old. She was born either in Kurima or Kurimka (small towns in Slovakia) then a part of the large Austro-Hungarian Empire. Mother was the oldest daughter of David and Esther Frankel (neé Orenstein).

The Zelczer family continued to grow and live in Vásárosnamény, Hungary, which, until the end of the first World War, was part of the vast multinational Austro-Hungarian Empire.

Surprise arrival in Ungvár: Me!

Unlike the other Zelczer children, I was not born in Vásárosnamény. According to my mother's two younger sisters, *Meemeh* (Aunt) Feigush and *Meemeh* Rózsi, my mother was pregnant with me in the summer of 1927, when she went "home" to her parents in Ungvár to attend the wedding of a younger sister Surtcha (Sarah) to Yecheskel Waldman of Stropkov. The Waldmans were a well-known and respected family who owned a small department store in the center of Stropkov, a mid-sized town in Czechoslovakia.

Mommy was not expecting my arrival for a couple of months and was not concerned about a trip of some 56 kilometers (35 miles) to Ungvár and back. She was determined to participate at her sister's wedding, and expected to return safely to Vásárosnamény in plenty of time to deliver her baby.

However, late on Friday night, I decided to enter the scene unexpectedly, and 'personally greet' my grandparents and the other wedding guests, two months before my anticipated due-date. In the middle of the night, Grandmother (*Bobbe*) Esther Frankel abruptly awakened her friendly neighbors, asking them to come and help locate a midwife to deliver a newborn. Bobbe even had to borrow diapers from neighbors and obtain some warm water and other supplies for my mother and for the newly-arrived, noisy intruder.

According to my aunts, my Zeideh (grandfather), David Frankel, took a lot of kidding that Sabbath morning from his friends in shul (synagogue). They all teased him ceaselessly about the new baby boy having been born to "him" so late in his old age.

My older siblings related that Mommy returned with me to Vásárosnamény about twelve days later. Given my premature birth, I had a number of health problems and developed boils all over my body. On recommendation of our Dr. Lengyel, I was bathed in a strong caustic solution. They had to bandage my eyes for protection against accidental caustic bath-spray. Twice a week, the doctor would pierce and drain the abscesses that covered my body. Undeniably — compared to those of to-day — medical knowledge and conditions for delivery of newborns were still very primitive in those years.

To help my anemia, Dr. Lengyel actually drew blood from my father's arm with a syringe and injected it directly into my veins. The relatively primitive state of medicine practiced those days permitted such drastic and risky treatment.

Timely advice

In 1930, the Hungarian economy was still in a state of turmoil and ongoing depression. The defeat in World War I and the resulting dismemberment of "Greater Hungary" was accompanied by serious political upheavals and instability. Materials and supplies for Father's leather business were expensive and hard to obtain. And, due to high unemployment, numerous people postponed their purchases of shoes, boots, slippers and handbags. Even much-needed repairs were often delayed. Business in leather-goods was poor and resulted in my parents' decision to get out of the leather business, once and for all, and open a bakery instead. "No matter what," they felt,

Telekkönyvi szemle

544.   *A)* **Birtoklap**   Vásárosnamény.
                    szám

Sor-szám	Helyrajzi szám	Az ingatlan megjelölése	Terület		Jegyzet
			kh	□-öl	
3.	358/89.	Szántó a Beltelekben:	–	209	
4.	358/88.	Szántó a Beltelekben:	–	51	

B) **Tulajdoni lap**

Sor-szám	Iktatószám	A tulajdonos és egyéb jogosult neve	Arány	Szerzési jogcím	Jegyzet
1.	4368/1930.	ifj.Balázs István és	1/2	vétel	} B.3—4
2.	"	felesége:Kiss Erzsébet	1/2	"	
3.	5956/1930.	Zelczer Salamon és	1/2	vétel	} B.13-17
4.	"	felesége:Frankel Laura	1/2	"	
3.	1472/1950.	Selczer Herman	1/5	öröklés	
4.	"	Selczer Miklós	"	"	
5.	"	Friedman Miklósné Selczer Helén	1/5	"	B.18.
6.	"	Selczer Szerén	1/5	"	
7.	"	Selczer Sándor	1/5	"	
8.	192/1952.	Magyar Állam	1/1	1952.évi.4.sz.tvr.	
9.	1317/1957.	Az ingatlan kezelője a:Szabolcs-Szatmár Megyei Tanács Mátészalkai Sütőipari Vállalat.			

C) **Teherlap**

Sor-szám	Iktatószám	A jogosult neve	Ft	f	Jegyzet
		T e h e r m e n t e s !			

865
......../1976.mksz.

Hitelenként záradék:Vásárosnamény,1976.március 19-én

Morvai Márta
előadó.

MÉN. OFTH. [611/a] rksz. TKV–1 számla 75.110 Pécsi Szikra Nyomda E-nnri

Recorded Land Deed for the Zelczer house and bakery.

Purchased by Solomon Zelczer and his wife Laura Frankel, in Vásárosnamény, Hungary.

Purchase date: Aug. 21, 1930.

"everyone needs to eat."

Furthermore, my grandfather, Eliézer Zelcer, had a long-standing and active baking business in Királyhelmec, so my father had the advantage of firsthand knowledge of the bakery business. He had spent a substantial part of his youth in his parents' home learning about operating a bakery, and the decision to now open one of his own seemed to be a natural step.

(An interesting aside, related to my grandfather's bakery in Királyhelmec: In Nov. 2010, while visiting New York, my wife Ruth became ill and had to see a local doctor for medical help. Waiting for our turn, we anxiously inquired at the desk whether Mrs. Zelczer's doctor had arrived. Overhearing us, an elderly woman with a walker curiously inquired whether we had any connection to the Zelczer bakery in Királyhelmec — because her older brother, Eliézer Katz, had worked there during the 1930's).

In addition to his family's encouragement, Father wanted his Rabbi's advice and blessing for such an important decision, involving his family's future livelihood. However, by this time, his long trusted counselor, the Keresztier'er Rebbe (1841-1925), known affectionately as *"Reb Sháyele Keresz-tierer,"* had passed away. My father therefore went to see the Rebbe's son-in-law, Reb Meier Yosef Rubin, who lived in the modest, picturesque town of Bodrogkeresztur (known as *Keresztier* in Yiddish), about 45 kilometers (27 miles) away. This type of personal business consultation was an accepted practice among various Jewish businessmen those days.

After my father told Rabbi Rubin about his difficulties in the leather business, his growing family's needs, and his alternative plan, the Rebbe advised him to go home and immediately order all necessary supplies and building materials for a bakery and a house for his family. Father rushed home and visited the brick factory and building-supply company of the wealthy Mr. Braun Layos. Braun's palatial residence, with its extensive, well-manicured and exotic flower garden on the northwest side of Vásárosnamény, was known far-and-wide as "The Braun Castle."

When my father told Braun's sales representative what he wanted, the man told him that someone had been there a short while earlier for the same purpose: to inquire about the purchase of building materials for a bakery. The clerk expressed his feelings that there were not enough potential customers in Vásárosnamény to support two new bakeries in town.

The Rebbe's advice came to father's mind, therefore he immediately placed the order for building materials for a modern two-oven bakery, a small bakery sales room, and a new home for his young and growing family. After his purchase of the building supplies became public, the other interested party gave up on his plans to build a bakery in town.

Zelczer Bakery

To complete this building venture, my parents bought the adjoining two corner-lots at 194 Rákocy Utca (street) and Vasut Utca No. 6, on the west side of Vásárosnamény. Mr. Vayna, the local architect who lived about a half a kilometer east of us, drew the blueprints for the building. He may have been the builder as well.

According to the date on a surviving copy of the recorded land deed, my parents purchased these two lots on August 21, 1930. Our new building was approximately one kilometer from the railroad station, and the same distance from the commercial center of Vásárosnamény.

We also rented a second store, a branch sales-store, in the center of town, where most of the large stores were located and the weekly "open-air-market" activity took place. Numerous vendors and farmers came to the open-air-market by horse- and ox-drawn wagons, bicycles, tricycles or on foot, from the many surrounding towns, bringing with them a full line of fresh produce, chickens, ducks, geese, fish, lambs and eggs for quick cash sales.

Our bakery's design was modern for its time. The double-decker wood-burning commercial baking ovens were neatly built into the east wall of the brick-faced workroom. The double-decker concept conserved expensive fuel, as well as space. The extensive bread cooling racks and the assortment of long, wooden "bread shovels" were lined up on the floor-to-ceiling bracketed shelves, all along the south wall.

The two commercial kneading-troughs (10x1.5x2 ft.) were in the second and larger workroom. The two heavy wooden covers for these troughs also served as workbenches for forming the various shapes of breads, challa, croissants, pretzels, kaizer-rolls, kifli, vekni, French breads and a variety of specialty rolls. The western area of this room served as storage space for general bakery supplies, including the various utensils and the tall white 50-kilo (110-lb.) cotton sacks of assorted types of flour.

Since gas for heating was not available in town, we used 40-inch-long cords of well-seasoned, air-dried wood, which were carefully stored in the nearby rainproof woodshed. It was the apprentice's job to bring in his open arms the split cordwood. He carefully placed them in the oven according to a specific air-gap and burning formula, and when he finished, the fire was finally ready to be kindled. After about an hour of heating the oven, the journeyman, the "master baker" in charge of the baking process, rolled up his sleeve and pushed his bare arm through the oven door to sense the temperature. He would then look thoughtfully at the long line of 'rising breads' in the baskets, and make the critical decision — was it time to begin the actual baking?

If the journeyman gave his nodded approval, the apprentice quickly closed off the dual chimneys with tight-fitting seven-inch-diameter steel caps (which they called a "tiply", a pot-cover). They would then carefully, but quickly, pull the gold-colored, still-burning embers and ashes from the oven with a specially designed 10-foot-long, flat-front, fire-scraping tool.

To get maximum use out of the glittering burning embers, they shoveled them directly under the large, rectangular, copper water-kettle, sitting recessed on the left side of the ovens. It was the duty of one of the apprentices to keep this 500-quart kettle full of fresh water at all times. A steady supply of hot water was essential in order to knead the various dough mixes and for cooking the salted, twisted pretzels. Additionally, the family often used this warm water supply for its own washing and bathing needs.

The journeyman, or one of the apprentices, immediately washed the bottom of the oven, removing the hot coal and ash-residue. For this job, he used a 14-foot wooden pole with water-soaked towels attached to its end. The next step was to place the well-formed and well-risen raw breads, challa, and other tasty items directly on the hearth of the oven. The men used polished-hardwood bread-shovels to place each round bread in the desired position. To accommodate extra-large breads, some shovels were about 16 inches wide and 18 inches long at their front end. Doing this correctly, speedily and without damaging the rising raw dough, was one of the many skills of a first-class experienced bakery team.

In 1940, at age 13, I started to help in the bakery for an hour or two each day. In addition, my mother would often give me a list of customers who owed us money for goods and services. I would make the collection rounds on foot and be back in two and a half hours with most of the cash. However, some customers gave me flimsy excuses and vague promises, such as, "I'll pay you... next week."

I liked doing this collection job much better when I was able to talk mother into letting me use the bread-delivery bicycle. That was a lot more fun. At my age, riding the bicycle on the street made me feel like a big boy.

My older sister Ruci was exceptionally skillful in the physical operation of the bakery. My parents often called upon her to manage and help in the bakery during the distressing worker shortages of 1939 to 1944. Additionally, Ruci and Mommy did the general bookkeeping and the daily upkeep of the strictly mandated "concurrent baking record," which was obligatory for governmental taxing purposes.

Our bakery, the Salomon Zelczer Bakery, was one of four in Vásárosnamény. The others were the Abrish Greenberger, Bóni, and Böhm bakeries.

The town of Vásárosnamény encompassed a large land area, and after some years, a number of our steady customers moved to remote parts of town and the distance became too great for them to carry their wares to us. To retain these clients, we would use our powerful horse, Gyúry, hitched to a light-grey tarpaulin-covered wagon, to do pick-ups and deliveries at a prearranged time from and to our preferred list of "regulars." It was usually one of the apprentices or I who did this job.

Our customers placed their freshly kneaded bread-dough in their flour-dusted, towel-lined carved-wood or wicker breadbaskets. When we picked them up, their breads were already at the beginning stages of fermenting and rising. We carefully baked their products, and in the early afternoon delivered their fresh crispy breads, along with the empty breadbaskets and their flour-laden towels. It is hard to describe the mouth-watering aroma of the freshly baked bread that filled the bakery and the whole backyard area. The delectable scent wafted into the nearby street.

Our charge for the baking, pick-up and delivery service was about 4 to 6 fillér (Hungarian pennies) per kilo (2.2 lbs.). This fee was certainly much cheaper than buying ready-made bread from our bakery because the customers often grew their grain in their own fields. Moreover, since they made the dough themselves, they saved the costs of kneading labor.

An additional benefit was the distinctive bread-flavor each household had for its own bread, due to its unique mix of varieties of flour, dough consistency, water content, sourdough proportion, and yeast.

As for the Zelczer Bakery, we also delivered our wide variety of fresh breads, rolls, horns, and pretzels to grocery stores. Most of our commercial customers were located in the nearby towns of Tiszaszalka, Tiszakerecseny, Vitka, Nyirmada, Jánd, Varsány and other small villages in our region.

The out-of-town deliveries to the grocery stores were usually made by my father because it was essential to have the baked goods arrive in good shape and to keep in personal touch with the customers. There was also the critical need to collect cash for merchandise delivered, as well as getting the customer's next order lined up for the following week's delivery. Superior goods, accurate orders, and timely delivery and collections kept everyone happy.

Trips with Father

In 1938/1939, anti-Semitic actions increased noticeably all over Hungary. Many sad stories of Jewish suffering circulated in the cities with growing frequency. We heard, with pain, how Jews were set-upon and cruelly beaten on the streets. There were reports that Gentiles overpowered Jews and forcibly cut off their beards or even tore their beards from their faces. In several instances, Jews were forced off public roads, and some were even thrown out of speeding trains.

Gentile children, teenagers, and even adults would often throw stones at Jews walking or traveling. Humiliating, and even life-threatening, harassment of Jews became a daily occurrence. Intolerance, hate and bigotry began to loom large and ugly over our lives.

The gendarmes and police turned a blind eye and a deaf ear to Jewish complaints. In fact, Jews often heard the gendarmes openly encourage Jew-baiters to file complaints against the Jews they had just attacked for allegedly starting the violence. Dirty tricks of this type stopped even the most courageous Jew from lodging a complaint against his assailant.

During these very sad years, my mother insisted that my father not travel alone any more. Consequently, one of the apprentices or I would get to travel with him to deliver the loads of baked goods to our customers in the nearby towns.

In my innocence, these journeys were always welcome news to me. They held the promise of new adventures and excitement and I looked forward to them. I also enjoyed these trips with father because we spent much of the travel time going over the *Chumash* (Pentateuch) and *Gemara* (Talmud) I had learned that week. We also covered the Hebrew translation of certain prayers or chapters of *Tehillim* (Psalms). Father was a good teacher, always speaking softly and very clearly.

I had the pleasure during these trips of hearing his lectures on nature, and he would often enlighten me about the stars, plant life, cleanliness and health issues. He knew much about animal life and cared greatly about the proper care of them, and was also quite knowledgeable and conscious of the physical world around him. He was a modern-thinking and forward-looking man.

On one particular ride at sunset, he quoted the *melámed* (teacher) of his youth who told him that the stars in the heavens are laid out in the form of the *Aleph-Beis* (Hebrew alphabet). He then proceeded to point to the heavens to show me a layout of some stars that vaguely resembled three or four Hebrew letters. I eagerly looked forward to future trips with him.

Father was mechanically inclined and liked to buy the best tools available for the bakery, as well as for the care of the barn animals. His interesting lectures on the physical world, on plants and animals seemed to shorten our shaky wagon trips, which otherwise featured observation of the panorama ahead.

I greatly enjoyed the occasional stops on the road to have our horse fitted with new horseshoes. Father was meticulous about the workmanship, and trusted only a few select black-smiths to work on his much-loved Gyúry. He often explained to me that an ill-fitting shoe would ruin a horse's leg in short order, causing pain to both the horse and its owner. "You must treat your animals with utmost respect and care," he would caution me. On occasion, he would quote me the verse from the Torah (Deuteronomy 11:15), from which our Sages inferred the command that we feed our animals before sitting down to eat our own meal.

My father would at first review the selection of iron bars on the blacksmith's shelf, and choose the one he wanted, based on height, width and quality. The blacksmith would then heat the metal in the open crucible and meticulously shape each custom-fitted shoe. I watched wide-eyed, enjoying the magical transformation of a rectangular piece of iron into a beautifully custom-fitted horseshoe. The new shoe included a built-in pair of replaceable threaded heels, as well as a gracefully-formed crown to protect the frontal hoof area. This hand-crafted design protected Gyúry's hooves from the daily hazards he had to endure on the long, stony road ahead.

I was already tall and strong enough to hold Gyúry's leg in my clenched fists and support it on my bent knee while the blacksmith repeatedly tested the fit and shape of the horseshoe. Finally, he would masterfully nail the new shoes to our horse's thick and healthy hooves, and we were ready to go.

I fondly recall the weekly bread delivery trips, especially on cold and snowy winter days. We would first stop in Tiszaszalka, then sometimes in Tiszaadony and then on to Tiszakerecseny. We traveled in our quiet, commercial-looking sled during the heavy snow season, while most of the year, we used the wagon with its four hefty, steel-banded wheels, which continually creaked as we made our way on the cobblestoned main highway. The 25-kilometer (16-mile) ride to Tiszakerecseny took a good three hours.

To keep our legs from freezing, we put them inside a heavy leg-sack, at the bottom of which we put several hot bricks to protect us from the bitter cold and wind. Sometimes, Yenta Friedman, the kindly mother of my brother-in-law, Mike, who lived in Tiszakerecseny, replenished our hot bricks for the return trip. With the wind blowing in our faces, and with the rhythmic ringing of the sleigh bell attached to the horse's reins, we enjoyed an exhilarating and exciting sleigh ride back home.

Mechanical interests

Sometime during this period, I became interested in the workings of mechanical devices and eagerly watched and observed any mechanic — carpenter, watchmaker, glazier or technician — at work. I loved to take things apart, and most of the time I even succeeded in putting them back together again.

Our next-door neighbor, the newly married and handsome Sándor (Shonyi) Schwartz, had an automobile and was an independent taxi operator. Whenever I heard him puttering around in his yard, I rushed over to watch him rotate tires, patch inner tubes and change engine oil. I tried to uncover the magic of how an automobile engine works.

In those days, cars had no starter, and I would cheerfully volunteer to hand-crank his car. In turn, he lent me several of his thin books describing the operation of a combustion engine. The small soft-covered books, written in Hungarian, explained how mixing the right amount of air with tiny droplets of gasoline creates small, controlled explosions inside the engine block, which are then transformed, by way of gears, into the turning of wheels and speedy travel. This amazing process seemed magical to me, and fascinated my young imagination.

Not knowing how my parents or siblings would react to my interest in automobiles, I decided to hide the books in the attic, well out of sight of my busy family. Whenever I could, I would quietly tiptoe up the stairs to the attic, where I would disappear and spend hours reading and re-reading those captivating books. After repeated absences from my daily chores and responsibilities, someone discovered my hiding place and tattled on me. I took a lot of good-natured ribbing for my early venture into mechanics.

Buildings on the spacious property

The Zelczer Bakery's storefront was on the north side of the lot, facing Vasut Utca. This two-kilometer long street ran from the railroad station in the west of town, to the central open-market area in the public square. Our family lived in the middle of the building, while the bakery was on the southern end. The wagon path from the side street was at the southern end of the property, outside and adjacent to the bakery wall.

A separate, small two-room building, with additional attic storage space, stood on our southern property line. These rooms served as sleeping quarters for the older children and as a living/sleeping area for the apprentices and the journeyman. I remember one journeyman Cháim Gerendásy and the apprentices István (Pista) Frankel of Nyirkarász and Mickey Weiss from the Nyirmada area. I recall the happy day when Mickey passed his master's tests and became a journeyman. We were all overjoyed for him. He continued to work at the Zelczer Bakery as a journeyman for a couple of years thereafter.

A quiet old man took care of the animals in the barn, cleaned the chicken coops and did small jobs around the house. Everybody called him *Bény Bácsi* (Uncle Bény). He worked for his food, clothing and shelter, and had no known family or friends. He was a reclusive person and chose not to eat with the family in the house. However, everyone treated him respectfully. I remember that when he passed away, my parents made the legal public-record arrangements and paid the fees for his burial in the Vásárosnamény public cemetery.

Attached to the west end of the hired-help's quarters was

Preparing a snack in the small kitchen of the Schwartz family. Circa 1942/1943. My older sister Edit, (Bina Rivka, rear left), is visiting her classmate & neighbor Elza Schwartz (with colorful apron, at right) and her two visiting cousins from out of town. Note the small, wood-burning cooking stove with the shining black stovepipe in the background, at that time considered modern.

the long woodshed, where we stored an ample supply of well-seasoned dry cordwood, with which we heated the two baking ovens. In inclement weather, the men would split the cordwood logs inside the woodshed, but when the weather was pleasant, they did so in the refreshing outdoor air of the backyard. The woodshed stretched westward for about 55 feet, all along the southern edge of the property.

An additional storage room near the barn contained hay, straw, corn stalks, several sacks of bran and other food for the animals. A manually operated fodder cutting machine, which we called the "*szecska-vágo*" (Hungarian), was also stored there.

The last building in the southwest corner was the barn for the animals, the horse-harness and various cleaning tools. In 1940, our animals consisted of one horse, one cow and an occasional calf, lamb, or goat. Our last two horses were named Yucy and Gyúry, and the cow's name was Muncie.

As the town had no central water system, we needed a reliable underground water supply. In the center of our yard we had a 36-inch-wide, concrete-lined shaft that extended from the water table, up to nearly four feet above ground. This open well supplied the water needs for the bakery and our large family. The water was cold, fresh and clean, and we needed lots of it for baking, cooking, dishwashing, laundry, bathing and gardening.

Carrying water was an unrelenting task, which had to be done daily, in summer's sweltering heat and during the winter's blizzard. Given the size of our family, we had three pails of fresh water, sitting on our kitchen's water bench at all times. Some of our neighbors, who did not own a well, came to our yard to draw water, free of charge.

In the northwest area of the lot was the vegetable garden that supplied our table with various fresh vegetables during spring, summer, and autumn. (See the complete list on the building plan page.)

Zelczer Family Bakery & Home
Vasarosnameny, Hungary
1930/1931

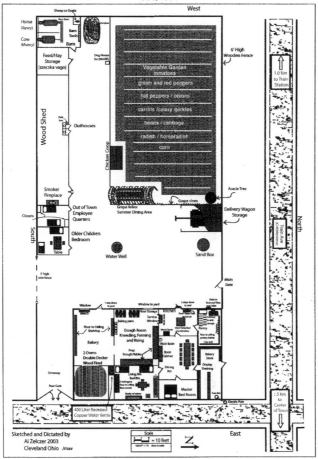

The onions, radishes, celery, cabbage and carrots we did
not consume during the summer were stored in our food cellar. To prevent shrinkage or spoilage, we carefully stored them
in moist sand, and they usually lasted throughout the winter.
We bought our seasonal fruits, watermelons, cantaloupes,

nuts, potatoes, beets, corn and beans from local farmers.

We also kept two wooden barrels of fine wine, one large and one small, in the food cellar. Every Friday eve, the teenage children took turns drawing a full decanter for the Sabbath table. I readily admit to having "accidentally" gulped a few extra mouthfuls of wine whenever it was my turn to use the red rubber hose to draw wine from the barrel.

At the front of the garden, in the northeast, was a tall grape trellis. In Hungarian, we called it the "*lugas*." During the summer, we ate the Sabbath afternoon Seuda Shlisheet (the third Sabbath meal), as well as some weekday meals, under its comfortable shade. Our house had electric power for lights, but there were no electric fans, central heating nor air conditioning.

In the other half of the yard, against the south side of the vegetable garden, we had a two-story chicken coop that housed our chickens, rooster, ducks, and geese. Further along was the doghouse for our beloved watchdog, Maxi.

A solitary, summer-blooming acacia tree was farther east toward the house, on the north side of the lot. The children liked to nibble on its fragrant tasty-sweet lily-white flowers, in spite of dire warnings from our elders that live bees or insects might be hiding inside these flavorful sweet snacks.

In close proximity was a seven-foot-tall wagon-shed, with six thick and strong wooden posts supporting the heavy, red, clay-tiled roof. This oversized space provided an open-sided parking area for our four-wheeled horse-drawn bread delivery wagon, as well as a covered playground area for children. A thick, waterproof light gray canvas was always securely tied to the wagon top, keeping it dry and clean.

Just off the kitchen we also had a year-round food pantry, which we called the *Shpeiz* in Yiddish. The stairway to the attic was in this small room. In the *Shpeiz* we stored a quantity of canned fruits and vegetables in tightly sealed glass and clay jars, which we patiently preserved throughout the summer and autumn. Some of these were stored for special occasions, such as upcoming holidays, or in case someone might take ill and could use a special delicacy to help his or her recovery. The *Shpeiz* also served as a general closet for winter coats, boots, brooms and miscellaneous cleaning items.

A supply of honey was also stored here, in a small, two-handled milk can. We used honey judiciously, as a topping on buttered bread and rolls, for baking honey cake, as a sweetener for tea and coffee if we were out of sugar, and occasionally to treat a cold or sore throat.

Hidden treasures in the attic

The attic was an extension of the food storage area and served to dry laundry during inclement weather. Here we stored commercial cotton bags of whole walnuts, along with dried apples and plums for the winter. A large, tightly covered wooden crate, which contained most of our Passover dishes and special serving utensils that we carefully packed away each year, sat prominently close to the top of the stairway.

To the right, in the far corner, was a smaller wooden box with a number of thick, heavy, hard-covered and expensive-looking accounting books. Each tome contained meticulously inked pages of customers' accounts, merchandise pickup dates, tax records, and balances due. The back pages revealed the uncollected — and uncollectible — sums long owed to the Zelczer leather business. All these were leftover records from our leather business days.

Strategically placed between the diamond-shaped roof tiles were several wire-reinforced clear glass tiles. They provided functioning light during the day, allowing me to spend hours browsing among the attic's hidden treasures and read books.

To my great astonishment, I once found two large handfuls of heavy one-Pengö silver coins hidden high up between the roof joists. This must have been a secret hiding place for my parents' emergency cash fund. I did not dare tell anyone about my clandestine find, lest my parents forbid my secret ventures into the attic.

Recreation and Sukkah preparations

A small rope-swing and a two-foot-high heap of blond-white river-sand provided fun and recreation for the children. The nearby scenic, but often perilous, Tisza River supplied the sparkling sand every spring. My brothers and I, with our friends, built many a sand castle in our yard.

During recess break in school, our "walnut-and-button" game was very popular. Most boys carried a small sack of buttons in their pocket. However, if we hit a losing streak, we sometimes had to replace our supply, by tearing buttons from our jackets and pants. We had a hard time explaining, and fibbing, about the missing buttons to our older siblings and parents.

In one mode of a button game, the winner was one that could precisely, correctly and powerfully 'strike' his button against a wall, such that it would bounce back and land close to another player's button sitting on the playground. He won the opponents' buttons if he could contact the sitting-button on the floor by means of his stretched handwidth; he lost the button if he could not make contact.

The walnut game consisted of a pyramid built of walnuts by one participant. Opponents took turns at rolling a steel ball-bearing and trying to knock the pyramid down. The loser paid the pyramid owner a nut if he missed. The winner gained all the nuts in the pyramid if he succeeded in knocking it down.

In the summer, we went swimming in the Tisza River with our *chéder* teacher or with other adults. Our house rule firmly stated that five people were the minimum for a swim session at the river, including at least one adult. The Tisza water was clean and fresh, but it tended to be fast-moving with many rapid undercurrents beneath its calm, silvery, shimmering surface. The swift and dangerous currents of the Tisza River, as well as the nearby smaller Kraszna River, unfortunately claimed the youthful lives of many unsuspecting swimmers and boaters.

Twice or three times during the summer months, a county fair took place on the spacious county grounds, featuring an open-air carnival and market, conveniently located just outside of town. All types of products were enthusiastically sold and traded, including low-priced clothing, rolls of dry goods, household supplies, toys, food, and alcoholic drinks of all sorts, as well as live fowl and an assortment of four-legged animals. The fair lasted a few days and was lots of fun for young and old. The varied shapes and colors of tents and the vast assortment of merchandise provided an attention-grabbing sight.

Several groups of local and roving Gypsy musicians performed a wide array of their music at the fair, such as their renditions of the Hungarian *Csárdás*, and happy and sad love songs. Every so often, they passed a collection hat down the lines of listeners and passers-by. A carnival atmosphere pervaded for the buyers, the sellers and the gawkers alike.

In the summers of our early teens, we excitedly went off with a group of older boys to watch the local football (soccer) games, played as a sporting rivalry between the athletic groups of the nearby towns.

The winters were long and hard, with lots of long-lasting and layered snow. We usually had plenty of opportunities for sledding, ice-skating and igloo-building, for both young and old.

During the *Sukkot* holiday (the Festival of Booths), we cleared the parking area of the covered delivery wagon and used it for our *sukkah*. My brothers and I eagerly looked forward to the fun of removing the sturdy red clay tiles from the roof, which we carefully stored in the nearby garden, and then heaving bundles of fresh and colorful cornstalks for *s'chach* (light vegetative roof covering) atop our new *sukkah*.

This was a true family affair, as we all had a great time decorating the *sukkah* walls, which consisted of a number of sheets of woven, soft bamboo shoots. It was great fun to attach the many multi-colored, multi-layered hand-made "stars", along with other special *sukkah* decorations. Our sisters excitedly hung the long looped chain decorations all over the inner walls and filled the bare spaces on the ceiling.

This happy *sukkah*-building event took place every year until about 1939, when bigotry, hate, and malicious anti-Jewish attitudes picked up momentum. Our daily life became steadily terrifying as anti-Semitic hooligans took to throwing stones at us on the streets and, into our *sukkah*, on our own property.

During this period of Hungarian history from 1939 to 1944, we no longer dared to complain to the gendarmes. As mentioned above, filing a complaint was more than likely to lead to a counter complaint being filed — and believed — against us. This form of harassment of Hungarian Jewry became widespread, and we were forced to live painfully with this new physical and political reality. For our personal safety after 1939, we built our *sukkah* inside the protected walls of our long woodshed.

Outdoor Plumbing

Yes, you have probably guessed correctly. We had a universally disliked, but quite necessary, family-sized "outhouse." Due to the needs of our large family and several employees, we were the owners of a deluxe, twin-style outhouse with a solid brick foundation.

Neatly camouflaged and discreetly built into our long woodshed wall were two toilet doors. One had to look carefully to identify the two openings in the middle of the tall wooden facade. The partially-hidden doors provided some degree of privacy during the daylight hours. One of the twin toilets had two cutouts, for children and for adults, and both had ample bench space to store large piles of cut-up toilet papers.

Quite visible were the deep candlewax burn marks near each toilet bench. These marks were made by the occasional nighttime user, holding a lit candle in his or her shaking, and often freezing, hand.

Multilingual and Multifaceted Lives

In the Yiddish-speaking world in which we lived, we called our parents Táttee and Mommy. Táttee would always call Mommy "Leebele" (affectionate for Leeba Málka, lit. beloved), and Mommy would typically call him "Zálman Leib," the Yiddish version of Yekusiel Yehuda.

During the six weekdays, the children spoke about 90% Hungarian. On Sabbath and holidays, if our parents heard us speak Hungarian, we were politely reminded, *"Heint is Shabbos/Yom Tov; heint redt men nor Yiddish"* ("Today is Sabbath/Holiday; today we speak only Yiddish.")

Given that both our parents were born during the era of the Austro-Hungarian Empire and grew up in the Slovakian/Hungarian/Ukrainian multilingual area, they spoke Hungarian, Czech, Slovak, German, some Ukrainian, and, of course, Yiddish. Furthermore, under the comparatively benevolent rule of Emperor Franz Josef in his pre-World War I days, most inhabitants of the Austro-Hungarian Empire, including the Jews, traveled fairly easily across borders and acquired several languages.

The Austro-Hungarian Empire was a conglomeration of many peoples. According to the New World Encyclopedia, its population was 24% German speaking, 20% Hungarian, 13% Czech, and the rest Polish, Ruthenian, Romanian, Croatian, and other ethnic groups.

One day I was surprised to hear my mother speaking German, while the visiting guests spoke an unfamiliar German-type language at our bakery. After they left, I found out that the visitors were speaking Flemish, while my mother spoke German; and yet, they understood each other. Dutch is also quite similar to German.

Vásárosnamény Jewry was proud of its large number of World War I veterans. A number of local Jews had even served in the select and very exclusive Hungarian "Huszár" Regiments, which Hungary often glorified as the best cavalry in the world. Among them were two brothers and a cousin of the Roth family. Scores of Jewish veterans were partially or permanently disabled. My half-sister's uncle and cousin were among the severely wounded. They were part of an unofficial World War I veterans' group that met socially and helped each other when needed.

About a quarter of Vásárosnamény Jews were either active in farming or dealt with the purchase and sale of various farm products. The others were tailors, glaziers, sheetmetal workers, teachers, grocers, butchers, bakers, and barbers. Others owned or ran candy stores, restaurants, delivery services, hardware and supply stores, tobacco stores, and bars. There were also watchmakers, wine producers, sales clerks, printers, physicians, soda-water makers, bookkeepers, scribes, veterinarians, carpenters, lawyers, insurance sales representatives, taxi drivers, and day-workers. Jewish homes were located all over the city — scattered among the homes of the general population.

Overall, after World War I and up to 1939, life in Vásárosnamény was quite hard, but still pleasant compared to

Vásárosnamény, circa 1940 —1941.

Relaxing against a ten-foot bale of hay in the Zelczer backyard are my older sisters Gitta (left) and Helen (center), enjoying the company of our Aunt Rózsi Frankel (right), visiting from Úngvár, Czechoslovakia.

neighboring countries. In Hungary, life was better and more secure for Jews than in most of its neighbors. The outstanding exception was Czechoslovakia where, from about 1919 to 1938, full democracy and freedom prevailed for all its citizens, Jews included.

During this short span of 18-19 years, all Czechoslovakian citizens enjoyed full freedom, opportunities to develop their skills, outstanding industrial growth and enviable prosperity. Sadly, it was precisely this success that brought about the country's downfall. We overheard adults explaining that it was "neighbor's jealousy" on the part of Germany, Hungary and Austria that did Czechoslovakia in.

The whole Czechoslovakian chronicle is long and complicated. However, the concluding consequence of this jealousy was that, with the full the support of Nazi Germany, Hungary attacked Czechoslovakia and annexed large portions thereof. This military action served nationalistic German interests in three significant ways:

a) It eliminated a thriving democracy in its neighborhood;

b) It brought Hungary closer to Nazi Germany and to its goals of dominating Europe;

c) It successfully enticed Hungary to join Germany in its protracted war against Russia.

Some of our neighbors were poor, and a few were quite wealthy, but the large majority of Vásárosnamény Jews lived a typical middle class life of the 1930's. Everyone worked hard and long hours to feed and clothe their families, while living in reasonably-sized homes for the times.

The Aryan Gentile population also had a small percentage of very poor, as well as a number of very rich, while perhaps 75% were large and small landowner/farmers.

Among the prominent landowner families in our town were the family of Baron Ötvös and the government-connected Máté family. They owned extensive tobacco farms and orchards, employed many hundreds of seasonal day workers, had many sharecroppers, and owned businesses around Vásárosnamény and elsewhere.

It is important to note that both my parents had many good friends among the Gentile population in and around Vásárosnamény. I heard no one talk openly about whether people were Jewish, Catholic or Protestant. The vast majority of people in Vásárosnamény were decent, law-abiding citizens.

Parents' education and training

As a young lad, father attended the Yeshiva of Reb Mordechai Yehuda Leib Winkler in Hegyaljamáda (*Máade*, in Yiddish), which was located in Hungary/Czechoslovakia. As already mentioned he left the yeshiva at age 18, and served a professional apprenticeship in Királyhelmec for three or four years, in the leather business of his elder cousin, Armin Kohn. He learned the art of leather design, paving the way for his entry into the leather goods and shoe, boot, and handbag design business.

Father was practical, smart, very polite, quiet and hard-working. He earned the respect of his peers and had many good friends. During his early years in Vásárosnamény, he was an active volunteer in the construction and management of the *Talmud Torah* (Hebrew school) and the new modern steam-heated *mikva* (ritual bath) building.

He would often repeat one of his favorite philosophical Yiddish sayings: *"Ven ess is nisht ázoy vee ich vill, vill ich ázoy vee ess iz,"* meaning, "When things are not the way I want, I want things the way they are." That became his personal motto for a life of peace and contentment.

According to mother's two younger sisters, *Meemeh* (Aunt) Feigush Waldman who lived in Tel Aviv and *Meemeh* Rózsi Rosenbaum who lived in New York, our mother attended public school in Ungvár beyond the basic six grades required by law at that time. This was because their parents, *Zeideh* (Grandfather) Dovid and *Bobbe* (Grandmother) Esther Frankel (nee Orenstein), insisted on a good education for their children, in both general and Jewish studies. I also heard from my aunts that Zeideh David regularly read the German language newspaper, as he was fluent in that language. Mother was active in the Ladies Auxiliary and in the *Gemilas Chesed* (charity) organization, to help the poor.

My parents had very fair work ethics. They would never degrade an employee, nor ask him to do more than they would do themselves.

They always conversed patiently, tenderly and lovingly with each other. I never heard an angry or loud word spoken between them. Mother was a well-educated, warm, outgoing, and pleasant lady. With the girls' help, she cooked healthy, nourishing and tasty meals. Her love, compassion and understanding for people were outstanding.

Father and mother were especially kind and considerate to the poor and downtrodden. Whenever a poor man or woman showed up at the door, Mommy would hand the person some cash, and never fail to ask, "Would you like to eat something warm? Or perhaps something cool?" I would often watch as Mommy served them at the table or instructed one of the older girls to do so.

Our meals were a family affair. Eating alone was frowned upon. After each weekday family supper, we *benched* (blessed) jointly the Grace after Meals, and father would then smoke his one-and-only cigarette of the day. Each day, one of the older boys had the honor of taking his turn to roll his daily cigarette, which father had patiently taught us to prepare on his tiny semi-automatic cigarette-roller. After we handed him the pack of kitchen matches, he lit his cigarette and sat at the head of the table until he finished it. No one else in the family smoked.

Preparing for Sabbath

On standing orders from Mommy, every Friday afternoon, in spite of our protestations, one of the older sisters took the eight-inch long scissors from the drawer of the foot-pedal sewing machine and trimmed the boys' *Péyot* (side hair locks). They were to reach no lower than the middle of our cheek-bones.

After that, the girls handed each of us boys a fresh set of underwear, a clean towel, a piece of homemade soap and 10 Hungarian fillér (10 cents). With these in hand we eagerly proceeded to the mikva (ritual bath) operated by the *Kehilla* (Jewish Community Council), where we first took a hot shower and then had the run of the two steam-heated, clean and refreshing indoor pools. This was a very rejuvenating experience.

To please the wide range and age of customers, one pool was extremely hot, and the second was just temperate. The concrete stepped pools were sunk deep into the ground, and were large enough to enable youngsters to give each other informal "swimming" lessons when the old-timers — the "interfering adults," as we often called them — got out of our way.

Upon our return home, the boys watched happily as Mommy and the girls finished their food preparations in the kitchen, which had begun quite early in the morning. The girls — Gittel, Chána, Sara Rachel, and Bina Rivka — set up the array of 18 Sabbath candles on the west end of the dining table, the *challahs* on the other end, and the dinner plates on both sides in between.

The boys ran all the last-minute errands. We shined our shoes and did the girls' remaining jobs. We emptied the two water lavers into the back yard garden area and filled the three water pails from the well, as more water was required on the Sabbath than during the week.

Before sunset, as Mommy was in the process of lighting the *Shabbas-lecht* (Sabbath candles), we gathered around Father and started our nearly 25-minute walk to the *Shul* (Synagogue), about a mile from our home. Unless some neighborhood adult joined us, Táttee would inquire about our week's public school or *chéder* (Hebrew school) learning activities.

On any given Sabbath Eve (Friday night), after our arrival from synagogue, Father and the boys sang in unison a lively *"Shalom Aleichem"* to welcome the Sabbath. He then filled his silver *Kiddush* cup to the brim, placed it into his cupped right hand, held it up, and chanted a melodious *Kiddush* (the Sabbath blessing over wine). The Sabbath meal was always a festive and formal occasion at which we were all dressed in our *Sabbath* clothes.

Father sat at the head of the table on the east end, and Mommy sat diagonally to his left, on what we called "the girl's side." This arrangement placed the girls closer to the kitchen, since they were the ones who brought in the delicious food from the kitchen, pantry and cellar and helped Mommy serve.

The boys sat on the right side according to age, with the oldest boy at home that week sitting next to Father. The employees filled out the right side and the western end of the table.

Our family custom was that after the first course one of the younger boys would go to the bookcase and bring two books of commentary on the *Torah;* the *Divrey Ávraham* and *Noam Elimelech,* and hand them to Father, who would then say his *Dvar Torah* (words of Torah) from one or both of them. When one of the older boys was home for the Sabbath, father would ask him to say a *Dvar Torah.*

The boys sang all the *Zmirót* (songs) listed in the *Siddur* (prayer book). The oldest boy at the table began the singing, and the others followed in turn. The songs tended to be hearty but not too loud.

Early Sabbath afternoon, after the large midday meal, Father would give us a short *"fárher"* (quiz) on what we had learned during the week. However, if any of our big brothers was home, Father would delegate the *fárher* to one of them. He would then take his Sabbath afternoon nap.

During the long summer Sabbath afternoons, our younger sisters and their local girlfriends would get together. Sitting in a semicircle on the shady, eastern side of the small house, they would sing beautiful Hebrew, *Yiddish*, and Hungarian songs to the delight of the rest of the family.

We, younger boys, together with some of our neighborhood friends, would often stop our ball-playing in the yard and gather around the girls to listen to their pleasing melodic renditions. Since we did not have a 'Victrola' or any type of plastic records, this was a great opportunity to learn the *Yiddish*, Hebrew and Hungarian tunes, to hear and memorize their intricate words, and to enjoy the girls' pleasant and harmonious voices.

This informal singing transmitted Jewish songs from generation to generation. We learned them by heart by repeating them over and over. This was the only available method to us in those days. These warm and sometimes very hot summer

Sabbaths were carefree and memorable.

On rare occasions, when reports of the motion picture then playing were favorable, Mommy would go with the older girls to the movie-house, located at the far end of Rákoci Utca, on a Sunday night.

Years in Chéder and Yeshiva

I was about five when I first attended the local *chéder* — three large rooms filled with boys ranging in age from 5 to 13. It was located on the large *shul* property, not far from the *Shecht-Shtibl* where we brought chickens to the *shochet* for kosher slaughter. It was owned and operated by the *Kehilla* (Congregation/Organization of the Jewish population).

I remember two full-time *melámdim* (teachers) — the elderly Reb Leib Eisderfer and his son Reb Moshe Eisderfer — with Reb Lippa and several other *melámdim* assisting them on a full and part-time schedule. Over the years, they did their best to teach us to read and write Hebrew and study various disciplines of *Torah* (Bible).

There was no organized Jewish school for the girls. The community's budget, or perhaps the prevalent old-fashioned custom of our *Kehilla* management, did not allow for teaching Hebrew subjects to girls.

Thus, parents had to solve the problem of their daughters' Jewish education on their own time and at their own expense. Parents who could not teach their own girls hired a part-time teacher for such skills as reading the *Siddur* (prayer book) and perhaps some basic Hebrew writing. As mentioned, we also attended the mandatory public school system for general studies five days a week, which were extended during my days, from six to eight years of study.

Long, rich school days:
Hungarian, Hebrew & Yiddish

On a typical weekday morning, my brothers and I left our house about 6:00, and started our walk to the *chéder* (Hebrew school) with our backpacks tightly fastened to our shoulders. During the winter season, when the early mornings were quite dark, we carried an oil lantern for our safety.

Dávening (praying) started at about 6:30. After that, we ate the breakfast we had brought from home at the same table where we *dávened* and learned. In order to make the best use of our meal-time, the *melámed* (teacher) read to us from one of the *Mussar* (ethics) books while we ate our breakfast. We then learned a bit of *Chumash* (Bible) with *Rashi's* commentary or a number of *Dinim* (religious laws).

We left the *chéder* just in time to reach the public school for our general studies which started promptly at 8:00. At 12 noon, the public school's morning session ended, and we walked back to the *chéder*. While we sat around the table and ate our lunch, (which we had also carried in our bags since early morning), the *Melámed* taught us *Chumash* and *Ráshi, Mishna* (oral tradition), or *Neviim* (Prophets). During this mid-day session, he sometimes squeezed-in some Hebrew writing lessons as well.

We had to finish these assorted Jewish studies on time, so that we could return to public school by 2:00 for more general studies, which lasted until our dismissal at 4:00 each afternoon. Once again, for the third time, we walked back to the *chéder* to continue with our Hebrew learning until about 6:00. After this full day of study, we walked home to eat our supper, do our homework, play and go to sleep.

We did have time off from Hebrew subjects on Friday afternoon after the public school session at 4:00, so as to provide sufficient time for Sabbath preparations. We had a full day off each Saturday, and on Sunday we concentrated on Jewish and Hebrew subjects. Sunday's learning was devoted to *Chumash,*

Ráshi, Dinim, Hebrew writing and *Talmud.*

Public schools in Vásárosnamény

For our general studies subjects, I, like all the other Jewish children in town, attended the government run co-educational public school, studying together with Gentile boys and girls our age.

In typical public school fashion, we sat on long, brown, wooden school benches. The boys sat on the right side of the room and the girls on the left side. Of the 44 students in my class, six boys and five girls were Jewish. Once we stepped inside the school building, we were not allowed to wear our caps.

We had a very good teacher by the name of Gyúla Hülber. He was strict and made us behave, but his classes were very interesting. He was usually easy on homework because he knew that all students had to help their parents with chores in the house and on the farm.

I do not recall Gyúla Hülber making any anti-Semitic remarks. Nevertheless, I do remember that he made facetious anti-baron and strong socialist-leaning comments. For example, he once said, "It's OK for Mr. Máté [one of the well-to-do moguls living in town] to charge more per kilo for his apples because he has many servants and therefore has greater needs for money than the rest of us. The small farmer, though, has no large expenses or servants to pay, and therefore he should sell his apples much cheaper, because his cash needs and expenses are much less."

I surmise that Mr. Hülber figured we would not understand his socialist remarks, and he would not get into trouble with the rich and powerful segment of society or the confrontational school principal, Mr. Yóska Gall.

Mr. Hülber was my teacher throughout the eighth grade in public school, and he taught us the full range of subjects —

except for religion.

Religious instruction in public school was a part of the government-mandated educational structure. Only clergymen of the "recognized denominations" had the right to come to public school to teach their religious beliefs and practices.

For Jewish students, Rabbi Kohn came to the public school to teach the required religious classes. However, on the days he could not be there, we were required to attend the Catechism Classes, strengthening Christianity. We had to partake in all songs and kneel with the class while saying the Catholic prayers led by the Priest. We had to listen to anti-Jewish tirades, prejudice, hatred, and long-winded curses for all other religions that "do not recognize their mistake and the urgent call to repent."

It was the firm decision of the Vásárosnamény *Kehilla* not to operate a Jewish Day School. The *Kehilla* leaders decided that rather than hire qualified licensed college-educated Jewish teachers to teach their children the general studies subjects, it would be better for us to attend the public school system.

Kosher tavern

Sholem Greenfeld and his wife Gizi Néni, (uncle and aunt of our half-sister Gittel), also lived in Vásárosnamény. Myrtle, Gittel's deceased mother, was a younger sister of Gizi Néni.

We always called her husband *"Sholem Bácsi"* (Bátchee), Hungarian for "Uncle Sholem." The Greenfeld's owned and operated a *kretschme* (tavern, in Yiddish) in Vásárosnamény. Sholem Bácsi was a disabled World War I infantryman who, due to severe war injuries, limped heavily on his right foot. He was substantially older than my father. I remember him as a short, but muscular, friendly old man with broad shoulders and a large chest. He had a combed, full white beard. Neat and clean, he always wore a fully-buttoned, dark, double- breasted suit and a long black-on-black matching necktie.

His war disability, which the Hungarians called *"Hadi-Rokkant,"* entitled him to a bar/tavern license issued by the Hungarian government. The government reserved most bar and cigarette-sale licenses for the numerous disabled World War I veterans — in lieu of paying them pensions.

The Greenfields' home and tavern was located on a spacious lot on the north-to-south main street, some eight houses north of the town's synagogue. The tavern/bar consisted of one large 25x25-foot room, which opened to a large backyard at its northeast corner. In the middle of the east wall was an entrance to the Greenfields' private residence, and on the west wall were swinging double doors which opened to the street. These wide-open double-doors were clearly intended to attract passersby for a drink or two, or preferably three or more, from among Sholem Bácsi's heady aromatic wines, and his wide assortment of pungent fruit whiskeys and liquors.

In the northwest corner of the room was a small booth for the bartender, divided off from the main hall by floor-to-ceiling wire-mesh fencing for the protection of the bartender, the cash accumulated, and the display of an assortment of alcoholic drinks. This was an open-view "bar-service" area, where the customer walked up to the window counter to buy his/her choice of wine, beer or whiskey. Home-cooked meals and sandwiches were also available upon request.

After the cash changed hands, the customer took his food and drink to one of three chestnut-brown wooden tables, flanked by matching painted wooden benches. Here, he shared his joys or sorrows with his buddies, while conversing, telling stories, drinking, eating, and singing aloud songs of love and patriotism.

Occasionally, for a small fee, one of Sholem Bácsi's friendly neighbors performed the "bouncer's" task and ejected a disorderly, inebriated or argumentative customer. Sholem Bácsi, his wife Gizi, their son Gedálya and their married daughter, Mrs. Gláncz, provided all the bartender services at the tavern.

Neither television nor stereo was available in those days. The Greenfelds did not even provide a "Victrola" phonograph record player, even though record players were available by then in some more modern establishments.

Greenfeld owned several vineyards in the sandy hills west of town, so they produced much of their multi-flavored wines. However, some of their specialty wines were bought from other producers.

Gedálya, the Greenfield's' middle-aged, yet unmarried son, had also served in the Hungarian Army during World War I. Like his father, he, too, was a disabled veteran. Gedálya had lost one eye during the war and had additional internal injuries not readily visible; this was the reason he was unable to get married. Their younger married son, Meier, worked as a Hebrew teacher in the nearby town of Cigánd and had a number of children. Their only daughter married a friendly and quiet man named Meier Gláncz, who was later to be my private Hebrew teacher. Not a single member of these war veterans' family survived the Holocaust.

Kehilla life: The Jewish Community of Vásárosnamény

For 33 years, Rabbi *Eliyahu* (Élias) Kohn was the government-recognized Rabbi of Vásárosnamény and its surrounding areas. He was in charge of the *Big Shul* (Large Synagogue) and was the only recognized Jewish authority in his extended district on all matters of Jewish Law and custom, such as *kashrut* (laws of kosher food), synagogue procedure, the *chéder* and baking *mátza* (unleavened bread) for *Passover*.

The *Kehilla* (Congregation) owned an extensive piece of real estate, on which stood the *Big Shul* in front and numerous Jewish community buildings. On the main street was also a small building where the *shóchtim* slaughtered cows, goats and sheep and the kosher butchers prepared the meat for sale. Halfway down the deep lot was a two-room chicken slaughterhouse, and further down was the *chéder* building with several large schoolrooms for the boys' studies with large playgrounds nearby. There were also houses for the families of Rabbi Kohn, the two *Shóchtim*, Shlómo Leib Berger and Yitzchak Elchanan Feldman, and the Rabbi's son-in-law, Reb Tzvi Hersh Lustig.

Near the front area of the lot was a modern, steam-heated Mikva building, containing a private bathing area for the ladies and public bathing areas for men.

The property had two wells. The well with a modern hand-pump was close to the Big Shul, and the open well was located toward the east end of the lot, close to the *Talmud Torah* building.

The *Kehilla* also owned the Jewish cemetery located on "Ilk Street," the long street leading to the next town called Ilk. The town also had a *Chevra Kadisha* (burial society), a *Bikur Cholim* society to visit and help the sick, and a *Gemilat Chassadim* group that provided charity and a free-loan society.

By 1937/1938, our town's Jewish population had increased significantly, both from local births and families moving in from nearby towns. The *Big Shul* no longer had enough room and the form of liturgy became an issue. The liturgy had always been *Nusach Ashkenaz* (Ashkenaz style prayers), but some members now desired to introduce *Nusach Sfard* (Sfard style prayers), largely used by *Chassidim*. For other members, the main consideration in wanting to start a new *shul* was to give the young Rabbi Lustig a leading position and help support his family.

Consequently, some 25 to 30 men joined to start a separate *minyan* (a quorum for prayer services) in the small *Beis Medrash*, which we called the *Small Shul*. Thus the *Big Shul* remained *Nusach Ashkenaz,* while the *Small Shul* started davening *Nusach Sfard.*

Rabbi Kohn appointed his son-in-law Rabbi Tzvi Hersh Lustig to be in charge of the *Small Shul.* This was a small one-room building about 100 feet east of the *Big Shul.* Rabbi Lustig was also in charge of the small Vásárosnamény yeshiva, whose enrollment varied from 12 to 20 boys. We liked him a lot, as he was a patient man and an excellent teacher and interpreter of Jewish sacred tradition.

This financial arrangement by which a Rabbi's son or son-in-law was appointed to head a yeshiva or a small synagogue was a common one and helped young scholars support their growing families.

The Zelczer family *dávened* in the *Big Shul,* until about 1938. Our seats were in the second row, on the right side of the synagogue, located right behind the *Mizrach* (East) row where the synagogue's well-to-do members sat. Sometime during 1938, we started *dávening* in the *Small Shul.* I do not know the reason for my father's change, other than to help the young Rabbi Lustig support his family. However, Mother continued to go to the *Big Shul,* since the *Small Shul* did not have a ladies' section.

Our Rabbi: Eliyahu Kohn

As mentioned, Rabbi Eliyahu Kohn was the spiritual leader of the Vásárosnamény community for 33 years, running all affairs of kashrut, Jewish education, the cemetery and more. He was the son of Rabbi Yaakov Yosef Kohn (Katz) of Ónod, a town near Miskolc, Hungary. He received as his dowry the rabbinic leadership of Vásárosnamény and a number of surrounding towns, when he married the daughter of Rabbi Shlómo Schreiber (Sófer), who was then the Rabbi of Beregszász, which is about 30 kilometers (19 miles) from Vásárosnamény.

In the 1930s, Rabbi Tzvi Hersh Lustig, Rabbi Kohn's

son-in-law, took over the management of the small yeshiva in Vásárosnamény, as well as the *Small Shul*. According to the provisions of his dowry, Rabbi Lustig was the designated Rabbi of Tarpa, a small town near Vásárosnamény. However, Tarpa had very few worshippers, not enough for either a *minyan* (congregational prayer quorum of ten men) or a livelihood for the rabbi. Therefore, Rabbi Kohn arranged for these two openings for Rabbi Lustig in our town. After World War II, I learned that Rabbi Lustig had written a book called *"Yedei Sófer"* (The Hands of a Scribe). He was a likable, friendly, good-looking and talented young man.

According to my information, Rabbi Lustig, his wife and their several children never returned from the deportation and cattle boxcar-train ride to Auschwitz-Birkenau. The Germans murdered them all.

Rabbi Kohn and his wife had several married children in Vásárosnamény and others that lived out of town. Of this large family, only the two married sons, Simcha Bunem and Ben-Tzion, and a daughter, Breindl, survived the Holocaust. However, even the two surviving sons lost their wives and about seven young children in the Zyklon-B poison gas chambers and the crematoria of Auschwitz-Birkenau. As for Rabbi Kohn, his wife and their younger children who lived with them in Vásárosnamény prior to the Holocaust — they were all murdered.

The salary for Rabbi Kohn, the *chéder* teachers, the *Shóchtim* and the *Shamash* came partly from congregation members and parents, and partly from the government-sanctioned Ecclesiastical Tax, which was an arrangement of taxes for religion, culture and education.

This law permitted each "recognized religious group" to tax all city dwellers professing adherence to its particular religion. These laws also forced everyone to choose a religion.

Anyone who was not on a "recognized religion" list was automatically taxed by the Christian Church.

Accordingly, all Jews were obligated by law to pay their proportional part of the Kehilla's expenses. In *Yiddish,* we called this tax the *Kultus-Shtayer.*

Hungary, like most other countries of Europe at that time, did not recognize a separation of Church and state. The government, together with the powerful Church, empowered the authorized Church groups to force the citizens of every locality to pay these "Church taxes" regardless of whether they wanted to belong to the Church or attend their services.

While these tax laws appeared to be an evenhanded governmental attempt to help all religions, they were actually intended to speed the Christianization of these countries. Given that most "minority religions" were not recognized, therefore, Seventh Day Adventists, Gypsies, Atheists, and sometimes Jews in smaller communities were automatically compelled to pay Church taxes to the Christian Church. Moreover, all minority religions were regularly intimidated and heavy-handedly "coaxed" to convert to Christianity.

Ecclesiastical Tax laws promoted the Church and provided lifelong job security for the clergy and church officials. The income covered the salaries and expenses for the vast number of priests, nuns, and members of the powerful political and ecclesiastic management. It helped the Church maintain and augment its vast real estate holdings, and amplified the expansion of its conversion and promotional activities.

In addition to the *Kultus-Shtayer,* every Jew in town had to pay to the *Kehilla* the *Gebelle,* a charge for the kosher slaughtering of fowl and animals. The *Shochet* would perform the kosher slaughter only after the prospective client handed him an appropriately priced, pre-paid *Gebelle* ticket. The *Gebelle* rate for doves was the lowest, and the rate for a cow and a bull were the highest. The fees for smaller animals and fowl were somewhere in between. There were two *Kehilla*-sanctioned

Gebelle ticket sellers in town.

Similarly, pre-purchased tickets provided admission to the well-kept, steam-heated *mikva* (ritual bath), also owned and operated by the *Kehilla*. The income from these varied services helped cover the upkeep and general expenses of all the buildings and property owned and operated by the Vásárosnamény *Kehilla,* as well as the salaries of Rabbi Kohn, Rabbi Lustig, the two main *melámdim,* the assistant *melámdim,* the two *shóchtim,* and the full-time *shamash* (sexton), Reb Ávraham Blau.

Besides for the general maintenance of Kehilla buildings, the duties of the *shamash* included waking up all Jewish families for the pre-Rosh Hashanah *Selichot* services by knocking on their windows with his long stick at about 4:00 in the morning. Similarly, he publicly auctioned off all the Aliyot every Sabbath and *Yom Tov,* and carried the *Kehilla's* official *etrog* and *lulav* to all Jewish homes during the *Sukkot* Holiday. I recall that during the war years only a small number of households purchased their own *etrog* and *lulav.*

Mátza baking for the Kehilla

Each year during the Hebrew months of *Kislev* or *Tevet* (December/January), the *Kehilla* accepted bids from any member in good standing to operate its *mátza* bakery for the upcoming Passover season. The reason for this early start was that it took time to line up the workers for this short-term business operation. To be fair to the bidders as well as the members of the synagogue, a purchase price for the wheat-flour was set in advance. This enabled the bidder to propose a guaranteed price per kilo at which he would sell the baked *mátza.* The *kashrut* of the milled flour and the baked *mátza* was under the supervision of Rabbi Kohn.

The successful bidder hired 10 to 15 women and girls for the strenuous job of creating a beautiful, evenly-shaped, round and thin *mátza* from each piece of the tough *mátza* dough. Rolling the *mátza* dough by hand was a difficult, back-breaking job. Nine hired men completed the remaining tasks to produce the evenly-baked *matzos* for the Jews of Vásárosnamény and the many smaller villages of the area.

The *mátza* baking oven was located inside one of the *chéder* rooms, while the other rooms were used for flour storage, kneading, rolling and storing the *matzos*. Therefore, the *chéder* was closed from about Purim to Pesach. The requisitioning of our *chéder* rooms for the *mátza* baking process created a very enjoyable and long pre-Pesach vacation for the *chéder* pupils. The children loved this added break very much, while our parents were not happy about it.

On the afternoon of Pesach Eve, the baking of the special *Mitzvah Mátza* (as the *mátza* baked that day was called) took place with great fanfare. At this special baking session, the enthusiastic, all-male *mátza* baking group proudly produced round, triangular and square raggedy-edged *mátza*. They happily baked away as they sang the appropriate chapters of *Hállel* (Psalms).

Private chéder teachers

In late 1936, some Vásárosnamény parents became unhappy about the deteriorating quality of teaching in the *Kehilla*-operated *chéder*. However, they had no other options, as this was the only official Hebrew school in town. My father got together with some of his friends and decided to hire a full-time private *melámed*. They searched high and low and hired an out-of-town teacher from the town of Hajdunánás for our group of 10-12 boys. He had the right credentials and displayed good judgment in doling out rewards for student accomplishments.

With the parents' permission, he set up an incentive system wherein the students who knew the allotted portions satisfactorily by Thursday night were rewarded with a pleasant three-hour swimming session at the sandy beach of the Tisza River on Friday morning. Those who did not pass the test had to stay home.

He also developed other contest-type incentive programs and his plan worked very well for a while. Unfortunately, after about a year, a certain serious predicament arose with him. The parents abruptly dismissed him for cause, and sent him home to his wife and children.

When I was about 12, I went to learn with another private *melámed,* Reb Meier Gláncz, who ran his own private *chéder/yeshiva.* He was the son-in-law of Reb Sholem Greenfeld, who ran the town's above-mentioned "Kosher Tavern." He was a good teacher and, as he had no children, was happy to use his spare rooms for our daily study classes. By the time I joined Rabbi Gláncz, our original private group had dwindled to about nine students.

Rabbi Gláncz divided us into two groups according to age. We learned *Chumash, Ráshi,* and pre-selected sections of *Talmud* tractates including *Bava Metzia, Eruvin, Avoda Zara* and *Kidushin.* We concentrated on learning sections covering fundamental laws pertaining to living the life of an observant Jew.

Vásárosnamény Yeshiva

When I was 13, my parents enrolled me in the Vásárosnamény *yeshiva* (School for Hebrew studies), where Rabbi Tzvi Hersh Lústig gave the daily *shiurim* (lessons). He was an excellent educator and under his skillful tutelage, we learned portions of the following *Talmud* Tractates: *Pesachim, Ketubot, Nedarim, Shabbat, Beitza, Sukkah, Avoda Zara, Bava Metzia, Rosh Hashanah* and *Gittin.*

These were segments of the *Talmud* pertaining directly to the observance of the *mitzvoth* (precepts) of daily Jewish living including the various holidays. Usually, he skipped the process of detailed rule-making, as well as most of the *ággadot* (homiletic parts) of the *Talmud*. No classes were given at night, and the *yeshiva* had no general studies subjects of any kind.

During early 1940, the student body consisted of 15 to 20 boys, aged from about 12 to 17. Three-quarters of them were local boys, whereas the others came from out of town. Private Jewish homes housed the out-of-town students, who took their daily meals as invited guests in different homes each day. I recall that our family, too, had several boys taking turns eating in our home on different days of the week. About 90% of boys went to work or enrolled to learn a trade, between the ages of 14 and 17, which explains why the Yeshiva student body was so small.

In 1941, the older *Yeshiva* boys (there was no such thing as married *Yeshiva* students) wanted to have their own *minyan*. They wanted to save *dávening* time and avoid the inflexible adult conduct and practices of both the *Big Shul* and the *Small Shul*. Reluctantly, the town officials gave them permission, and a separate *Bachurim minyan* (boys' quorum) was organized in the *chéder* building.

During the Purim season of 1941 or 1942, the older students produced a play called *"Der Yosef Spiel"* (The Joseph Play). It was a dramatization of the *Torah's* account of the travails and successes of Joseph, whose brothers sold him to the Midianites, who sold him to Ishmaelites, who sold him to the Medanites, who sold him to Potiphar, in Egypt, and finally, the story of his aging father, the Patriarch, Jacob. The boys performed the play without fancy scenery or music, yet it carried its forceful message most effectively.

Der Yosef Spiel was very popular, and the public eagerly paid the entrance fee of 20 Hungarian fillér per person. It provided the older boys with some pocket money that helped them with their food, clothing and general needs.

Express Friday-night
Bar Mitzvah preparation

The preparations for my *Bar Mitzvah* celebration were typical for my friends; they were straight-forward and rather simple. I well remember the Friday night before my *Bar Mitzvah,* when my father instructed my older brother Baruch to help me prepare to read the *Haftara* (the "Prophets" portion) the next day in shul.

Bar Mitzvah boys in our Yeshiva had to learn to chant clearly and loudly the several blessings before and after the *Haftara.* We recited the *Haftara* itself somewhat quietly — not out loud with the proper cantillation, as is prevalent in many communities.

The preparations for the in-home celebration were equally brief. On Shabbat morning, Mommy and the girls arranged the table with several plates of delicious honey cake and sponge cake. They then patiently waited until after *dávening,* when about a dozen friends of the family stopped at our house to wish my parents and me *Mázal Tov.* They would then share a tumbler or two of slivovitz (plum brandy), take a couple of pieces of cake, and with this, the *Bar Mitzvah* celebration was over. This was the typical preparation for a businessperson's son's *Bar Mitzvah* celebration.

The *Sófer* (scribe), Yehoshuah Zorach Goldberger, produced my new set of *Tefillin* (phylacteries). He had been a classmate and good friend of my father in the Yeshiva of Máade many years earlier. Mr. Goldberger lived in Hajdunánás, about 45 kilometers (28 miles) from Vásárosnamény.

❧ **2** ❧
Life Changes in the Shadow of World War II

Emperor Franz Joseph and the Habsburg Empire

To understand the political situation of Hungarian Jewry prior to World War II, it is important to begin with Emperor Franz Josef, a descendant of the well-known, and traditionally anti-Semitic, royal Habsburg family. The Habsburg dynasty ruled the Austro-Hungarian Empire from about 1526 until the end of World War I, about 1918/1919. Franz Josef's rule stretched from about 1867 until his death in 1916.

His vast empire included Austria, Hungary, the Czech regions of Moravia and Bohemia, Slovakia, the southern part of Poland known as Galicia, much of Ukraine, Ruthenia, about half the Romanian region of Transylvania, Bosnia, Herzegovina, Serbia, Croatia, Slovenia and a part of what is today Italy.

Although he was cruel to Jews much of his early life, nevertheless, in his middle-to-later years, Franz Joseph adopted policies which related to Jews in a fairer, more benign manner and began acting more humanely toward Jews. However, when it came to providing (partial) compensation for the extra taxes and punishing assessments that he and his predecessors had squeezed out of the Jewish communities, he would not return cash to his Jewish subjects, but rather proposed to build them schools and synagogues. Unfortunately, internal politics and religious disagreements among the Jews frustrated his belated friendly intentions.

In a history on Hungarian Jewry, *"Toizent Yur Yiddish Leben in Ungárn" (A Thousand Years of Jewish Life in Hungary)*, Yekusiel Yehuda Greenwald writes in detail about Franz Josef's extraordinary efforts to finally emancipate the Jews after centuries of spurious promises made to them by the various Habsburg rulers.

One of the crucial changes at the end of World War I was the dissolution of the Austro-Hungarian Empire and, therefore, the end of the Habsburg monarchy.

Hungarian Communists:
My family was left with nothing

Following World War I, in 1918/1919, gangs of Communists roamed numerous areas of the former Austro-Hungarian Empire. After a number of political machinations, movements of military units and the murder of key political figures, the Communists managed to take control of Hungary for a short time. Following summary court-martials by kangaroo courts, they conducted many private and public hangings.

As a result, large portions of Hungary fell under the tyrannical rule of the Communist leader, Béla Kun, and his Communist-Socialist regime. In typical Communist fashion, the new leadership openly robbed people of their personal belongings on the streets and in their homes, stores and warehouses. Complete chaos and anarchy reigned throughout the country, as murder, mayhem and robbery were daily occurrences foisted on a helpless population by the roving Communists and their rag-tag army of sympathizers. They summarily killed many thousands.

I was about 13 years old when Mommy was reminiscing one day, telling us about how the Communists behaved in Vásárosnamény. She related sadly how they smashed the shuttered door to our home and lined up the young Zelczer family against the wall. The family then consisted of my parents and four young children.

"The Communist gang threatened our family with their hatchets, steel pitchforks and butcher knives," my mother said, "threatening to chop all of us to pieces if we tried to stop them from loading all our possessions, even our personal clothing and all our food on their wagons."

The Communists, known as Béla Kun's "Red Army," made my parents' choice rather easy. The alternatives were either to lose all their possessions and remain alive or to lose their possessions *and* their lives.

The family stood lined up against the wall, shivering and sweating, while the gang proceeded to remove everything from the house and the business. They took all raw materials, the ready-made leather goods, and all the machinery from the nearby Zelczer leather supply business. My family was left with nothing.

After months of political infighting and violence, the "White Army" of Hungarian Regent, Admiral Miklós Horthy, managed to overcome the Communists late in the year 1919. Horthy killed many of them in the process and somehow restored order in Hungary. Béla Kun speedily disappeared from the scene and fled to Romania.

Interestingly, Miklós Horthy insisted on being called "Admiral," even though Hungary had neither a Navy nor even a seaport. He also styled himself "Regent," to give his rule the appearance of being a legitimate continuation-regime of the Austro-Hungarian monarchy, although he was in fact a benign military dictator.

A short time after World War I, the Treaty of Trianon, signed in France on June 4, 1920, harshly punished Germany, Hungary, the Habsburg Empire and their partners for having started the war. The pact called for a re-distribution of about 72% of the former Greater Hungary and awarded large land areas to Czechoslovakia, Romania and Yugoslavia. The victorious countries and the League of Nations enforced the new land allocation.

An exhausted, badly beaten and greatly shrunken Hungary embarked on rebuilding itself, amidst the pain, human misery and monetary losses. Shortly thereafter, the economic situation in Hungary worsened even more, as the long and bitter worldwide depression which gripped all of Europe, rapidly enveloped Hungary as well.

With great difficulty and hard work, my parents managed to get back into the leather business, but on a considerably smaller scale. However, since the four-year-long war had consumed almost everybody's cash, many of their past and potential customers could not afford to buy the goods offered by the Zelczer leather business. Indeed, standards of living dropped severely and everyday life became distressed. It was then that my parents decided to enter the bakery business.

Children flee in face of war

During August/September of 1938, there was a story in town that the Hungarian Government was getting ready to attack Czechoslovakia, with the implicit approval of Nazi Germany.

To start such an action, the Hungarian Army needed to move thousands of soldiers, by foot and bicycle, closer to the Czech border. The two Vásárosnamény-area rivers — the smaller Kraszna and the larger Tisza — had several important bridges leading towards the Czechoslovakian border.

My parents had noted the steady increase in the numbers of soldiers marching or goose-stepping through town. They tried to interpret those army movements and make an educated guess regarding the possible effects on our family.

By 1938, most Hungarian newspaper and magazine editors had allied themselves with the government, wholeheartedly supporting a pro-German, pro-Nazi, and anti-American political stance. The newspapers conveniently "forgot" to print anything about the Army movements, knowing that publication of Army movements might set off an alarm, and alert the Czech government.

Adding it all up, my parents became frightened that an imminent war might break out right in our backyard, as Vásárosnamény was only about 26 miles from the Czech border. To get us away from this possible war area, they sent the four youngest children, of whom I was one, together with my oldest sister, Gittel, to my mother's uncle and aunt, Moshe and Chaya Beilush. The Beilush family lived in the city of Nyirbátor, some 28 miles in an opposite direction, and therewith they doubled our distance from this possible theater of war.

The five of us lived in Nyirbátor for about a month. We had a wonderful time getting to know our Beilush and my second cousins the Schwartz family, and enjoyed their exceptionally friendly and warm hospitality. The Rosh Hashanah, Yom Kippur and *Sukkot* holidays of 1938 still stand out in my mind, as this was my first occasion to enjoy them out of town. It also provided us the pleasure of listening to the pleasing voices of our two Schwartz cousins, as they sang with a five-boy choir at the *Chassidic Shtibl* (synagogue) where *Fetter* Moshe Beilush *dávened* (prayed).

Eventually, Hungary, with the encouragement and political support of Germany, attacked Czechoslovakia in a series of small border clashes, starting in November 1938. These attacks were launched by Hungary, despite the fact that it had already managed to tear away parts of Slovakia and Ruthenia from Czechoslovakia under the terms of the "First Vienna Awards."

Hungary quickly repaid Nazi Germany for its help by tightening up on all dissidents, embracing Germany's anti-Jewish policies, and promulgating new anti-Semitic decrees against its own Jewish citizens. Later it allied itself with the Axis Powers (Nazi Germany and Fascist Italy) in the war against the Allied Powers: Soviet Russia, Great Britain and the United States.

Hate speeches against all minorities and dissidents became fashionable, and each group of bigots out-performed the other with its accusations and lies.

Hungary hastily started the process of identifying and revoking citizenship rights of those it suspected to be of Polish and Czechoslovakian ancestry. Therewith, the Hungarians stripped their own countrymen of civil and human rights, confiscated their property, and sent them off to concentration and annihilation camps in Poland.

The Hungarian government and population confiscated the Jewish-owned farms, real estate, homes, personal property, animals, businesses and licenses. The general population eagerly accepted the government action against the Jews.

Growing anti-Semitism all around us

The ill winds of seething anti-Semitism in Germany spread a novel disease and untold pain onto all of Europe. The human environment became poisoned, and unimaginable actions began to take place openly and publicly.

National radio stations incessantly screamed anti-Semitic songs, and anti-Semitic articles in the newspapers increased in length, frequency and venom. Hungarian Army soldiers shouted newly-composed anti-Jewish songs as they marched on the streets. In numerous ways, Hungary became an enthusiastic, full partner of Nazi Germany.

This turn of events deeply marred our love for Hungary. We could not grasp this transformation, as this was our country and we had always been proud Hungarians. This was the country for whose freedom our fathers and grandfathers had given their blood, their limbs, and their very lives. All of the anti-Semitic developments terribly upset our communal and family life.

And, this was not the end. In an abrupt move, the Hungarian government suddenly demanded that all Jews prove their Hungarian citizenship, retroactively to the year 1800 — or earlier. These records were to be found only in County and City offices, and even there, documentation was scanty to nonexistent.

Very often, known anti-Semitic officials withheld public records which could prove such citizenship and would release them only upon payment of exorbitant "under the table" bribes. Even then, there was no assurance that after receiving his payment, the officiating anti-Semite would keep his promise and deliver the legal papers.

Most citizens could not afford to raise the funds for the bribes. As a result, in case after case, the Hungarian officials simply annulled centuries-old citizenship rights.

Beginning in 1938/39, and until our forced deportation and final imprisonment in the Beregszász Ghetto in April, 1944, Hungarian Jews were publicly degraded and violently assaulted. We were attacked everywhere: at the railroad stations, on the streets, in our houses of worship and in the city hall. The assailants faced minimal risk of punishment at the hands of the law enforcement officials.

In 1940, Hungary officially joined the Axis Powers' Tripartite Pact of Germany, Italy, and Japan.* This event marked the final abrogation by the Hungarian authorities of even a semblance of civil rights and justice for Hungarian Jews. The parliament passed many anti-Jewish laws and enacted additional restrictions to the anti-Semitic *"numerus clausus"* (Jewish quota) laws. The threats against us became unbelievably harsh. Systematically, the government and media turned our life and existence from bad to worse.

On a Sabbath during the Jewish High Holy Day season of

---

* The Axis Powers included Germany, Japan, Hungary and, in varying forms, Italy, Romania, Bulgaria, Turkey, Vichy-France, Slovak Republic, Yugoslavia, Croatia, and Finland. Among the Allied Powers were the USA, Russia (USSR), and Great Britain.

1943, the Vásárosnamény police chief came to our house with two armed assistants and ordered my father, "Open the bakery, immediately! You are to start baking right now!" My parents had no choice but to open the bakery on the Sabbath and bake bread on our holy day. I remember that Sabbath well. It left a terribly bitter memory for a long time.

Indeed, political times had changed so badly that my father, a lifelong law abiding, taxpaying citizen, was ordered by police officers to work on the Sabbath, violating both his religion and his personal will. It was unbelievable. We were all hard-working, productive and registered citizens of our country. My great-grandfather was born just 64 kilometers (40 miles) from our house and was a loyal citizen of his country. Yet, here was the chief of police, an official public servant, forcing Jews to violate their religious beliefs — just to enrage us and prove our utter helplessness.

We had become a defenseless minority, and this episode was just one more example of the methods by which the city officials demonstrated our utter subjugation. Radios, newspapers and political speeches spread a whole line of vile anti-Semitic falsehoods. Jews had become the natural and visible scapegoat for all of Hungary's ills. All the war expenses, deaths, casualties, materials and food shortages — the Hungarian government managed to blame them all on the Jews.

It would seem that such deep hatred, discrimination and bigotry against Jews had been inculcated into the population from early childhood. Although, in earlier times, anti-Semitism seemed to be generally dormant in all but a small section of the population, it now surfaced and exploded into the public arena, together with the advent of the Hungarian Nazi Party, known as the *Nyilas* (Arrowhead) Party.

The new laws restricted Jews from dealing in certain government-controlled products, such as tobacco. Jewish doctors, lawyers, and engineers were allowed to practice their profession only where no Gentile was available to serve the public. Jewish workers were brusquely dismissed from all public service positions, and often from private jobs as well.

All at once, contrived charges against Jews began to crop up — a constant reminder of our tenuous situation in Hungary. Non-Jewish neighbors and fellow employees invented "actionable" stories in order to cause a Jew's job, license, house, farm, business and cattle to be taken from him. Such actions prevented large numbers of Jews from earning a living. Jews became unemployed and were abruptly reduced to begging.

This situation was not only due to the active anti-Semites and Nazis. The persecution of Jews, and the Holocaust itself, was made possible by the fact that a majority of decent and reasonable Gentiles sat on the sidelines, while the noisy minority of hate-filled bigots spat at us and abused us, whenever and wherever we appeared.

In addition to purging Jews from the world of commerce and industry, the Hungarians began pressuring for the eradication of all so-called "political opponents." These included Gypsies, homosexuals, lesbians, Slavs, Romanians, other minorities, and whomever they called "racially foreign" peoples.

Levente Szolgálat:
Paramilitary training at age 12

The Hungarian National Defense Law required all male citizens, age 12 and older to complete about four hours of paramilitary training each week. This workout continued until about ages 18-21, when induction into the regular army took its place. The Hungarians called this military-prep schooling the *"Levente Szolgálat"* (Pre-Military Service). While we wore our civilian clothes during training hours, it was mandatory to wear our military-issue caps on our heads. The military exercises were held on public school property and on the municipal football field.

During my first year, our *Levente* training consisted of drills with wooden replicas of the long Hungarian Army guns that had fake wooden bayonets attached to their ends. We began to learn the rudiments of proper use of gun-sights, and how to accurately aim at the target. We drilled marching and singing patriotic army songs. We practiced these skills with Aryan and Gentile boys our age. Girls were exempt from *Levente Szolgálat*.

Pre-Military Training/Service, cir. 1941/1943

One of the Vásárosnamény Jewish Levente Szolgálat groups, with picks and shovels — instead of guns — with which to perform unpaid construction work. My older brother Bernát is in the center (head circled) behind the boy in the center foreground. An unfriendly Hungarian Army Officer with a loaded pistol (left) is directing the Levente Szolgálat "labor detail."

By the year 1941, the Hungarian government deemed the Jewish boys to be untrustworthy of learning guns — even wooden copies of guns. However, to humiliate and abuse us further, we were now made to march through town with shovels, picks and axes on our right shoulders. We were forced to do various menial tasks on a variety of digging projects all around town — without pay, needless to say.

If it was raining, or if the ground was muddy, our trainers — the Army officers — took extra pleasure in ordering us to lie flat in the mud while wearing our own clothes, and forcing us to pretend that our shovels, picks and axes were rifles and guns. We had to pretend-shoot at an imaginary approaching enemy, with the earth-digging implements in our hands. Throughout the so-called instructive course, the official trainers expressed a heavy dose of undisguised anti-Semitism.

I also remember one particular year when a sudden blizzard and swirling winds created 12-foot-high snow banks along the main route to the next town. The Levente officers ordered us to work 12-hour daily shifts to clear the mountains of snow — by hand.

This unpaid snow-clearing labor was not required of the Aryan and Gentile youths in the *Levente* service. They sat out this particular winter storm warming themselves by their home fireplaces with their families.

Ostrich politics and psychological denial

Starting around 1938/1939, the Hungarian Government put out of business all newspapers which tended to take an opposition approach. The government-sanctioned newspapers and radio stations automatically supported Nazi-Axis policies, as well as the anti-Semitic positions taken by the Hungarian government. This rendered them obviously unreliable as news sources for Jews, leaving us bereft of and hungry for accurate, reliable sources of information. Consequently, during those anxious years, whispered rumors were our only source of "reliable news."

Later, in the Beregszász Ghetto, beyond the critical, constant struggle for food and survival, rumors, both good and bad, became the essence of our daily lives. At times, these rumors gave us some hope that we might live another day, or even make it to freedom

When we were taken to the Ghetto, the rumor was circulating that due to the shortage of farm labor, the Hungarian Government would send us with our families to tend the extensive fruit orchards in central Hungary, the well-known Hungarian "fruit basket," located around the area of the city of Kecskemét.

These early rumors seemed reasonable; given that the Hungarian Army was busy fighting the war alongside Germany and the Axis Powers, and the general population was busy producing armament and war supplies, therefore, there was a need to force all the Jews to help produce food for the Hungarian and German armies and for their civilian populations.

Strange as this may seem, some considered this good news. They reasoned that even if we would not have enough bread to eat, we certainly would have fruits and vegetables — or at least their peels. As a whole, we took heart from the fact that forced relocation to the Kecskemét area would take us further away from the possible war-fronts on the Slovakian and Polish borders.

Of course, this was all wishful thinking on our part, and we really had no way of ascertaining if the Kecskemét rumor was true or not.

The reality was that the Nazi leadership and their Hungarian partners were clever, and knew how to keep us off-balance with all kinds of rumors. They fully understood our need for information, so they cleverly disseminated false rumors to keep us content and hoping, no matter how ambiguous the rumor might be.

Unfortunately, our local as well as our national Jewish leaders were deceived by such simple ruses, just as they had been in prior years when bad news of Polish and Ukrainian Jews arrived. Some people referred to this approach of our leaders as "ostrich politics."

For example, starting April, 1942, within a short period of about seven months, Slovakia deported 60,000 of its Jewish citizens to concentration and murder camps in Poland, Germany, Ukraine and one in Czechoslovakia — Therezienstadt.

We now know that there were many detailed warnings of the Nazis' Master Plan to obliterate European Jewry; they called it the "Final Solution." Good, reliable people, such as Rabbi Michael Dov Weismandel, Gizi Fleischmann and others, passed these warnings on to the Jewish leadership of Hungary, as well as to the Allies and the Vatican, but to no avail.*

A small number of courageous individuals managed to escape from the mass-killing fields of the concentration camps of Poland, Ukraine, and Czechoslovakia, bringing with them first-hand eyewitness accounts of the mass murders. (No doubt, there were additional unsuccessful escape attempts; sadly, they can never be counted as, typically, no one would be alive to tell of them).

In 1942, Hungary was still a safe place for its Jewish Hungarian population, but not so for runaway Slovakian Jews or other non citizens. Our family, too, underwent some escape experiences.

In the summer of 1942, our aunt and uncle, Sarah Rachel and Yecheskel Waldman, of Stropkov, Czechoslovakia, were hiding in field caves, barns and basements to get away from the mass deportations.

As hiding became more difficult, they had their two young boys, Boruch and Michael, smuggled to their grandparents in Ungvár and to us in Vásárosnamény, Hungary, for temporary safekeeping. The boys' three younger sisters were also successfully smuggled across the border into Hungary and hid at

---

* See: *Min Hameitzar,* second edition, Emunah Publishing, pages 105, 106, 109, 151, etc.; *The Nazis' Last Victims,* by Randolph L. Braham, with Scott Miller; pages 57-101; *Eim Habanim Semeichah,* by Y. S. Teichtal, Kol Mevaser Publications, Israel; pages 49, 50, etc.

various times in the Frankel grandparents' home in Ungvár and in an orphanage in Budapest, Hungary.

In the autumn of 1942, we could no longer hide our two young cousins. The insurmountable problem was that the boys could not speak Hungarian, and we suspected that our prying neighbors were ready to betray us to the Hungarian gendarmerie. My parents arranged to smuggle them to Ungvár, where they joined their three younger sisters and parents in short-lived safety.

Tragically, early in 1944, the Hungarians decided to deport the Ungvár Ghetto to Auschwitz-Birkenau. Our aunt Sarah Rachel and all her five children were murdered upon arrival; only their father, Yecheskel Waldman, somehow, survived the Holocaust.

Károly Szécsi, our "Righteous Gentile"

One of the best wholesale customers for Zelczer Bakery's fine baked goods was Károly Szécsi, the owner of a rural General Store in the picturesque, tree-lined farming town of Tiszakerecseny. Tiszakerecseny had a population of approximately 900 and was located about 25 kilometers (16 miles) from Vásárosnamény, a good three hours' ride by horse and wagon.

Mr. Szécsi was an exceptionally good human being, with a warm and friendly disposition. He was a cheery, nimble, and strong-looking man with a light, ruddy complexion. His family consisted of a hard-working, attractive wife and several lovely teenage children. When Mr. Szécsi served his customers, one could see on his face his genuine pleasure at serving others. His lively Hungarian expressions generated a smile on the face of his listeners as they rolled out of his mouth. He always wore a ready and pleasant smile.

His store was quite popular and had a long list of steady, satisfied customers. He regularly bought our whole line of breads, rolls, salted pretzels and other baked goods wholesale and then sold them to his patrons.

Over the years, a deep and true friendship developed between my father and Mr. Szécsi. When I followed Father into Károly Szécsi's store on my first bread-delivery trip to Tiszakerecseny, I became keenly aware of their deep comradeship. I saw their eyes meet and their faces light up, just like two brothers meeting after a lengthy separation. They seemed sincerely happy to see each other, exchanging warm greetings and a friendly handshake.

Mr. Szécsi was a good and reliable customer for many years. Over the years, he learned the Jewish holidays, especially Passover, when he would not be able to buy from us given that the Zelczer Bakery was closed for all Jewish holidays.

A very strange thing happened during Passover of 1944. It was a lovely spring day, and in typical holiday fashion, Mommy and my sisters set our dining room table for a festive meal with a white tablecloth, porcelain dinner plates and a wine-filled decanter at the head of the table. Our family was about to sit down for the holiday noontime meal, when Szécsi Károly showed up at our home, unexpectedly.

Mr. Szécsi arrived with a large wagon-load of hay, drawn by two well-groomed, light brown horses. My father must have sensed that something was wrong. "Why are you coming here on Passover?" he asked Mr. Szécsi in distress. "You know very well that we don't have bread during the Passover holiday!" Whereupon Mr. Szécsi nervously answered that he did not need bread, but wanted to meet privately with him and my mother.

They went into the back room, where Mr. Szécsi confided that he had heard from reliable sources of a secret plan to deport all the Jews from their homes. He had therefore quickly loaded his wagon with hay, leaving a hollow area inside the hay. Mr. Szécsi offered to conceal our family inside the hollow area and take us during the night to his farm and hide us there.

My parents did not know what to make of this information and how to react to this potentially catastrophic development. They had no reliable way of assessing the risks to themselves, or the potential risk to their good friend Mr. Szécsi and his family for his extremely generous, yet perilous, offer. They decided to ask him to wait a little, while Father would go to seek advice from our religious leader, the elderly Rabbi Eliyahu Kohn.

About an hour and a half later, Father came back and told Mommy that the Rabbi advised not to go, but rather to stay in our house. The Rabbi and my parents relied heavily, and wrongly, as it turned out, on our Hungarian citizenship rights, which seemed to them rock-solid and irrevocable.

My father told Mr. Szécsi of their decision, thanking him profusely for the information and his generous offer. Sadly, and somberly, Károly Szécsi went home without any members of the Zelczer family hiding in his hay-wagon.

However, my parents gave Mr. Szécsi some of our cherished possessions: Sabbath candelabras and some family heirlooms, including a silver *Kiddush becher* (wine goblet) given them by Grandfather David Frankel, Mommy's gold wedding and diamond rings, and some other items. He took them back with him to Tiszakerecseny for safekeeping "until these troubles blow over."

This exceptional man represented a small part of humanity that did both — displayed singular courage, and practiced the best of human conscience.

Nearly a year later, upon regaining my freedom in 1945, I returned to Vásárosnamény. Hearing of my homecoming, Mr. Szécsi invited me to his home in Tiszakerecseny for a sumptuous family dinner, where he gladly returned to me all the Zelczer family valuables that had been entrusted with him.

(See below: "Károly Szécsi revisited").

I am certain there were many good-hearted, concerned Gentiles around, but most became invisible and inaudible, and very few were prepared to take the high risks that Károly Szécsi did. To this day, I do not know how many other "Szécsi Károly's" bravely offered refuge to their Jewish friends in the Vásárosnamény area.

Without doubt, Mr. Szécsi was one of the "Righteous Among the Nations" and an exemplary human being. He made that trip to Vásárosnamény on his own initiative and was prepared to take an extreme risk to himself and his family. He offered help and hope to a friend at a time when anti-Jewish hatred and barbarism were prevalent all over Europe. Mr. Szécsi had the moral courage few others of his countrymen displayed.

German soldiers arrive

It was early March 1944, when we first noticed several pairs of uniformed German soldiers with small side arms on their belts, nonchalantly walking the streets of Vásárosnamény. They gave the impression of being on vacation in a friendly neighboring city. In harsh reality, however, by Mid-March of 1944, Hungary seemed to have willingly melted into Nazi Germany.

In the following weeks, our very survival hung in the balance. In early April, a barrage of additional anti-Semitic laws was presented and passed by the Hungarian Government and the (National) Socialist Parliament. Among them was an edict ordering all Jews to wear external identification. The directive was quite precise. *"A yellow star, 4.5 inches tall and wide must be worn on the left side of the chest, together with an armband of the same size and color, on the upper left sleeve of any outer garment."*

We were ordered to wear these "Jewish identifications"

whenever walking or appearing on any public street, convey-
ance, park, or building. A Jew caught on the street or in any
public area without a yellow star and yellow armband was
subject to a heavy fine and/or prison confinement.

Apostate Jews, who either themselves or their parents had
many years earlier legally converted to Christianity or other
faiths, were also obligated to wear a distinct identifying mark:
a white star and armband the same size as our yellow one, on
their chest and sleeve.

The consolidated government control of all media and the
Parliament enabled the Hungarian Nazi demagogues to sway
the Hungarian people, primed by years of anti-Semitic propaganda and hatred, into going along with their criminal
policies.

With the official passage of the new anti-Semitic laws, the
lives of the approximately 825,000 Jewish citizens of Hungary
— including 100,000 converts now identified as Jews — profoundly changed.*

The message of the Nazi Hitlerites and the Arrow Party's
drive throughout Europe was that the destruction of Jews — as
well as Gypsies, political opponents, homosexuals, and the
feebleminded and chronically ill — would solve all problems.
However, essentially, this merely disguised their conspiracy to
rob and despoil all non-Aryan peoples and repress their do-
mestic political opposition.

Expulsion orders announced on street corners

I believe it was on Sunday, April 16, 1944, the day after the
Passover holiday, that the Vásárosnamény "Town Crier," an
officer of the court, with his ever-present bone-gray drum suspended from his shoulder, made one of his characteristic "legal news circuit announcements" going around the entire

---

* See: T.D. Kramer, *From Emancipation to Catastrophe*; 44, Univ. Press, 2000.

town. His announcements changed our lives beyond recognition. Nonchalantly, he read from typewritten pages the latest official government rules and regulations for all citizens to hear.

Among other minor township news of the day, he announced the following dreadful messages:

a) The Hungarian government herewith orders all Jews of Vásárosnamény and the surrounding towns to leave their homes and present themselves at the brick factory in the city of Beregszász, (about 30 kilometers away).

b) Before going to Beregszász, all Jews must first go to the official assembly point, at the castle of Mr. Layos Braun, a local Jew.

c) The Jews are permitted to take along food, clothes and all personal belongings — but not more than what the family members can carry by hand. Everything else must be left behind.

d) All of the above must be carried out, on pain of arrest, fine and prison confinement.

We were stunned. With these simple words read aloud by the town-crier, the government expelled us from our homes and stripped us of our citizenship and human rights.

We could not understand it. It did not make sense to us. Our ancestors lived in this region for hundreds of years, industriously helping to build up this country, settle the land, create commerce and work opportunities, and since that time we lived our lives as proud Hungarian Jews. And it all was to end in banishment and disenfranchisement.

Our parents knew no way out of this predicament. They told us to start packing, and select what we felt was important to take along for the undefined trip. My brother Bernát was 20 years old; I was 16½. We were each able to carry one backpack and two handbags containing clothing, bedding and food. My parents, my younger brother, and three older sisters, who were home at the time, carried lighter packages with similar contents for the eight of us. We hastily managed to sew into our clothes some valuables and cash, for whatever trials and tribulations might befall us along the unknown road ahead.

Eight pieces of silk: The Gray Silk Shawl

Before we left for the assembly point at the Layos Braun castle as per the Hungarian Government order, Father urgently requested all of us to come into the large back bedroom. We immediately filed in, one by one, and stood before him in distress with our pale blank faces. With a striking, severe and pained look on his face, Father walked over to the two, floor-to-ceiling, mahogany linen-closets. He angrily swung open its polished double doors, and bent over considerably to reach the rear section of the deep center shelf.

From behind a stack of ironed and neatly folded white bed linen, he pulled out an elegant Gray Silk Shawl from its long-time hiding place. He slowly turned around, and with measured, long steps, rejoined us at the front of the room. When he stopped, he unfurled a delicately fringed shawl, which I had never seen before, and held it high in the air to keep its trailing tasseled end from touching the wooden floor.

With swift movements, he pulled from his right pants pocket his razor-sharp pocketknife. He opened its cutting blade and proceeded to slice the shining but aged silk shawl into eight pieces, each a handbreadth wide. Starting with Mommy, he handed each one of us a strip of the shimmering shawl.

As we silently stood around him, intensely perplexed, he announced in a low, somber and pained voice, "This is a *Kamiah* [amulet] from Reb Sháyele Kerestier'er. Always keep this with you, and it will help safeguard you." (Rabbi Yesháya Steiner (1851-1925) was a long deceased, well-known religious leader whom Father had favored.)

He then put the eighth piece of the Gray Silk Shawl and his ivory pocketknife into his own pocket.

Life in the brick factory Ghetto

A couple days later, on April 17 or 18 of 1944, the Hungarian gendarmes, wearing their official headgear with tall rooster feathers, took charge of our forced push into the Ghetto of Beregszász. Tired from the heart-wrenching and sad wagon-trip from Vásárosnamény to Beregszász, the eight members of my family dragged our meager supply of food, bedding and personal clothing into the Beregszász Ghetto grounds.

Our family consisted of my father Solomon (Yekusiel Yehuda), age 56; my mother Laura (Leeba Málka), 48; half-sister Gizi (Gittel), 31; sisters Szeréna (Sara Rachel), 23, and Edith (Bina Rivka), 21; older brother Bernát (Baruch), 20; myself, Alex (Yesháya), 16½; and my younger brother, Josef (Sholem Yosef), age 12.

Some time after World War II, I found a dated record concerning my older brother, Bernát, at the Yad Vashem Holocaust Museum archives. It records him as having been among those taken from Auschwitz-Birkenau to the Buchenwald concentration camp, on Jan. 23, 1945. His group arrived from the Auschwitz-Birkenau concentration camp in Buchenwald, after a forced winter "death-march."

As for the additional members of my family, my oldest brother, Herman (Gavriel Tzvi), age 29, served for a number of years in the Jewish Labor-Battalion section of the Hungarian Army, known as the dreaded "Munkatábor." This was a network of infamous anti-Semitic army labor camps in which the Hungarian Army treated the Jewish labor battalions with incredible cruelty. One example: The Jewish "Munkatábor" soldiers were forced to clear minefields for the Hungarian and German Armies by walking, arm-in-arm, and shoulder-to-shoulder, through suspected minefields, without prior training or protective equipment.

Another older brother, Miklós (Yisrael Mordechai), age 28, and an older sister, Helen (Chána), 26, were at this time (early 1944) working under false "Aryan" names in Budapest. They were thus able to avoid being forced into the Beregszász Ghetto with us. Nevertheless, they too wound up in concentration camps.

Official Yad Vashem record of my older brother Bernát
Zelczer's captivity in the Buchenwald Concentration Camp
system. He arrived on Jan. 23, 1944. His birth date is shown
as Feb. 5, 1924. He is listed as a "Hungarian- Jewish"
political prisoner #120166, and is further identified as
having come from Auschwitz.

Our Ghetto, actually a huge outdoor security prison, was in the large storage yard of a brick factory, located outside the city limits of Beregszász. This fenced-in forsaken area served as "living quarters" for the innocent Jews from *Bereg Megye* (Bereg County), Hungary, and was the first step in our terrible confinement.

We were forced into this brickyard by the thousands — including the ill, lame, aged, wounded Hungarian Army Veterans, pregnant women, newborns and children of all ages.

There were hardly any men of military age among us since for the past 3-4 years nearly every able-bodied Jewish man had been drafted into one of the many infamous Munkatábor regiments. The few military-age men among us either had had special job-related exemption permits which the Hungarian government now revoked, were on sick-leave and arrested on the streets, or were captured by police while in hiding.

For family living quarters, the gendarmes assigned us the bare outdoor areas under the brick-drying sheds. Previously, the brick factory had used these areas to protect their brick and cement blocks from sun, rain and snow.

These sheds had no walls and were wide open on all four sides. They consisted of six to eight seven-foot-tall poles and sturdy upper crossbeams supporting a sloping clay tile roof. Four to six families, with members ranging from the very old to newborn babies, were jammed into each of these open sheds. There were rows upon rows of them.

We spent our days and nights on the wet, cold and rough grounds. The floor of our restricted area consisted of raw earth sprouting scraggly wild grass and poison ivy and was strewn with broken bricks, pieces of concrete and glass. Those who "lived" close to the edges of the sheds were exposed to the morning and evening sun, the wind and the frequent cold spring rains.

There were no tables on which to put our meager food, no chairs to sit on, and no beds to lay down our weary bodies. At night, only the thin blankets that we had managed to bring with us from home separated us from the bare ground, the harsh grass and the moist soil. Here we slept by night and spent our days with feelings of utter degradation. This barren, dirty spot of earth was our "home" for about five weeks.

There were no washing or cleaning facilities. To wash up, we used a bucket of cold water — the only kind available — while other family members held up a sheet or blanket for a modicum of privacy.

Like prehistoric nomads, all families slept outside on the raw ground, on thin blankets, in one large encampment. The lack of privacy between parents, children and neighbors, further taxed our mental state.

Those who were able went around the decrepit brickyard helping mothers with their howling and hungry children and tending to the dire needs of the grief-stricken, the veterans, the infirm, and the aged. We helped in the kitchen to prepare some meager food and brought it to the indigent. The availability of food and health supplies was woefully inadequate.

The tension in the Ghetto showed clearly on the faces and in the demeanor of the people. One could readily see the sullen, angry and confused faces and the pressures that built up in them. A mixture of controlled fury and desperate hope was visible in the eyes of the elders. There was no detectable way to get the families out of this predicament and no apparent way to combat this well-organized evil. By this time, my parents too, were unable to help our family.

We did not know what to expect from minute to minute. However, the Ghetto presented a picture of utter brutality which gave us an inkling of what we could expect from our captors. This shattered our understanding of so-called "normal human behavior." The Hungarians and Germans perpetrated unimaginable abominations. This was the beginning of our mass dehumanization which served to make it easier for the Nazis to line us up for mass murder. Once we were inside

Hinda, daughter of my brother Herman and Aranka
(nee Kleinbart) Zelczer. Hinda (born 1941?) and her
beautiful young mother were murdered upon arrival
in Auschwitz-Birkenau during May-June of 1944.

the Ghetto, we became incredibly isolated and estranged from
our own country, Hungary, on which we had depended for our
safety.

In spite of my determined efforts in this chapter, the miserable conditions in the Beregszász Ghetto are simply beyond
description.

Run? Stay? Agonizing life decisions

The Beregszász Ghetto (brick factory yard) was located a few kilometers outside the city limits. New Jewish families were forcibly brought in daily from towns and cities throughout Bereg Megye, taking the place of others who were deported earlier in cattle boxcars. The number of Jews in the Ghetto was said to have fluctuated between 3,000 and 9,000.

At this late juncture, our fleeting thoughts of resistance, escape, or simply easing our daily mode of life failed, for the following reasons:

1) Armed Hungarian gendarmes surrounded us 24 hours a day.

2) There were only a small number of adult Jewish men in the Beregszász Ghetto, because nearly all able-bodied, army-age Jewish men were by now serving in the Munkatábors.

3) We had no guns, nor any other type of weapon, nor were we trained in self-defense or attack operations.

In short, we really did not have a fighting chance. By the third day in the Ghetto, our difficulties had mounted beyond our capacity to deal with them intelligently. Just attending to our basic bodily needs — water, food, health, medicine, sanitation — as well as the cold nights, rainy and windy days, the babies and the feverishly-sick crying for medicine and food and the total uncertainty regarding our future had exhausted us physically and mentally. Sitting on the dirt floor and standing outdoors all day had taken its toll on our worn-out bodies and frayed nerves. Only our teenagers and adult volunteers were able to extend help.

One day, the Hungarian gendarmes offered to issue a limited number of "volunteer work permits" for men or women who were willing to do physical labor outside the Ghetto in nearby Beregszász. They offered a small amount of food, such as two half-kilo loaves of bread as payment for 10 hours of hard labor.

We were suspicious of the offer, fearing it was a trap to grab and capture the small number of able-bodied young men and women amongst us. However, we had no way of knowing the truth. We had to rely on doubtful information planted by the Hungarians or the Germans. These bits of hush-hush and semi-secret information were only available to us by way of rumors and the grapevine, which we wryly called "HGZ", standing for the Yiddish words *Hab Gehert Zugen* (meaning, "I've heard it said...").

One HGZ rumor had it that the Hungarian gendarmes and the German guards were pocketing the money the factories paid for our labor, and that was the reason they so zealously tried to get us to work there. That they possibly took the money for themselves did not matter to us; since we were hungry, the offer of bread did appeal to many of us.

Additionally, this offer opened a small window of opportunity for some daring "volunteer workers" to escape, by hiding during the workday, and then making a run for their lives during the night, and disappearing somewhere in the Beregszász countryside.

For those workers who contemplated taking this risk, the work offer became an extremely agonizing decision. At stake was an indefinite separation from their beloved families, as well as their very lives and safety.

To be more specific, a husband, father, sister, son, daughter, or brother who received a work permit for work in the city of Beregszász and wished to then run away had to deal with a host of weighty considerations:

* He or she could easily be killed in the process...

* He or she might never see their family again...

* The Germans or Hungarians might retaliate against remaining family members in the Ghetto...

* The escapee's family might find itself in need of help, and the escapee would not be available to help them...

* The Hungarians and Germans could decide to move their family out of the Ghetto or even out of the country, leaving the escapee with no knowledge of the families' whereabouts...

Ultimately, the HGZ rumors had it that between 20 and 40 people volunteered for the work. Apparently none of them were able to actually escape the Ghetto, as they were marched under close guard by the Hungarian gendarmes to and from their work areas. I had no personal contact with any of them, but it was said that they did receive the small amount of bread offered for their work.

Their deception worked

After we were taken to the Beregszász Ghetto, we soon realized that we had become a special type of isolated prisoners. We were terribly frightened, painfully aware of the shocking loss of our freedom, our citizenship rights, our human rights and our civil rights. We had no access to our homes, our cash, our land, our animals and our personal belongings, which we needed for survival. The only real possession we still had was something very precious: our family sitting beside us on the dirt/grass floor.

We were distressed by our total helplessness and the grim realization that we had no life-saving choices. We were physically, mentally and monetarily unable to plan an escape with any reasonable expectation of success.

Regardless of all the indignities we were forced to endure, the vast majority of those in the ghetto tried to think rationally and keep calm, maintain their faith and keep alive their hope. For lack of any other assurance, we had to take comfort in the old saying, "there is safety in numbers" — even in a miserable ghetto.

There were some unconfirmed stories that a small number of individuals overcame the obstacles and managed to escape. Of course, we had no way of determining whether their escape was successful or whether they were caught and sent to jail or to the murder-camps and fields in Poland or the Ukraine, or perhaps were summarily executed.

The days of spring 1944 melted into one another, both in their appearance and in practice, so that we hardly knew or cared what day of the week it was. We were constantly hungry for some nourishing food. We felt the Hungarian-German noose tightening around our necks, as we became more helpless and vulnerable.

The multitude of persecution methods, the selective expulsions and the group murders that started in 1939 had now developed into Hitler's "Final Solution" and became the dominant Europe-wide Nazi policy. We became powerless beyond any description.

We reached the point where we very much wished to believe the false rumors fed us by our German and Hungarian tormentors, and we earnestly hoped to be sent to the Kecskemét area in Central Hungary to do farming and raise food for the anti-Semitic Hungarian nation. *Their vicious and well-planned ruse had worked.*

Hungarian cattle boxcars to Auschwitz-Birkenau

But it was not to be. We were not going to be taken to Kecskemét, but to Auschwitz-Birkenau. It was only a question of when. Several factors determined the speed of our deportation:

1) The towns and cities were limited as to how many farmers they could line up to help deliver Jews to the Beregszász Ghetto.

2) The national Hungarian railroad could furnish only a limited number of lockable cattle boxcar trains.

3) As large as it was, Auschwitz-Birkenau was physically limited in the number of victims it could "process" — that is, suffocate to death — at a given time. It was similarly limited in the number of victims it could burn each day in its round-the-clock crematoria.

We were not to remain in the brick-factory/ghetto for long. Suddenly, after being imprisoned there for about 5 weeks, its railroad tracks seemed to come to life with sounds of crackling railroad ties and blaring hoots of a steam-engine. We became intensely aware that a line of Hungarian cattle boxcar trains had pulled up to our area of the brick-drying sheds.

Without warning, a platoon of Hungarian gendarmes, accompanied by several German SS-men appeared from behind the line of boxcars. One by one, they lowered their bayonetted long-guns hanging from their shoulders, placed them on their hips in a typical stabbing-attack position, and aimed at us.

The gendarmes shouted an order at us: We had ten minutes to pick up our scattered personal belongings and makeshift bedding from the ground, place them in our suitcases and line up at the railroad track to board the cattle boxcars.

Before pressing us into the cattle trains, the gendarmes demanded all our cash, papers of ownership, wedding bands, rings, necklaces, gold and all jewelry. They threatened to shoot on the spot anyone caught withholding valuables or disobeying their orders.

With an array of guns pointed at us, this was clearly not an order we could ignore. Without a sound of protest, we all lined up — a confused, frightened group of worn-out, wretched unfortunates.

The terror was overwhelming. Fear-ridden young children clung to their frightened mothers' skirts, and babies screamed incessantly in their mothers' quivering arms. It was a terrifying sight.

Most of us unloaded nearly everything, except for the items previously sewn into our clothing or hidden away in our shoes. However, some people took a chance and retained various valuables.

The decision of our adults to comply with the orders was painfully difficult. Their deep fear of collective punishment against women, children, the elderly and the infirm, stifled any thoughts of resistance. Parents made sure their children behaved and followed all orders quietly.

Despite our compliance with their orders, the gendarmes singled out a number of elderly women and men for truncheon beatings, simply to add another measure of fear and terror. It was difficult to observe and impossible to grasp how our own Hungarian Government could be behind such cruelty against its loyal citizens. Perhaps the gendarmes wanted to show off their expertise in cruelty to the German SS standing beside them, as they drove us mercilessly into the cattle boxcar trains.

It was not clear to us whether the gendarmes were planning to share this robbery with the grinning pistol-armed German soldiers standing by. In any event, the gendarmes continued to carry away bucketfuls of our cash and valuables.

It was only at this late stage that most of us realized that we were not going to do any farming in Kecskemét. We felt utterly abandoned and betrayed by everyone: our towns, the police, our Gentile neighbors, and the political leaders of the treacherous Hungarians. These barbaric, indeed monstrous acts brought us to hate the entire Hungarian nation with few exceptions.

With our whole family standing together in the firing line, we were unable to defend ourselves. We had absolutely nothing to match the bayonetted guns of the brutal gendarmes. All the while, they continued pointing their loaded guns at us while cursing us and rushing us to overfill every cattle boxcar.

By the time the train doors slammed shut on us, we actually felt somewhat relieved, knowing that the Hungarian gendarmes could no longer hurt us, and we were safe from their rifle butts and the abuse. It was impossible for our senses to comprehend what was happening to us, let alone to make any sense of it. The fear that our siblings or parents might be killed... had us paralyzed.

Our minds raced in all directions, but there were no solutions on our horizon. By this time, we fully realized that we had lost our last options. They shipped us off like blinded cattle. We could not see and did not know anything of our destination ahead.*

Peepholes in the cattle boxcars

After the Hungarians locked us in the cattle boxcars, they apparently attached us to other freight trains carrying cattle, coal, lumber and the like. They certainly were experts in knowing how to demean us and take our humanity away. The conditions inside the cattle boxcars were beyond human endurance, but endure we did.

Before the gendarmes slammed the door shut, they gave us two water buckets. One contained potable water. It did not last long among the crowd of thirsty, frightened people. The second bucket was for use as a toilet. Imagine — one open bucket for all 70-to-90 of us. We had no choice. Males and females, the adults, the infirm, and children, were all jammed together with no privacy. The lack of basic facilities was overwhelming and caused us to look at each other with mortification and guilt. The overcrowding and lack of sanitary conditions caused a stench that formed a nearly palpable haze inside the cattle boxcar.

---

* According to post-war reports, of the 435,000 Hungarian Jews deported to death camps, only about 35,000 survived.

We were sometime able to peek through the peepholes in the boxcar and see the names of the railroad stations we were passing. Adults familiar with the geography of the region told us that we were not headed in the direction of Kecskemét. "We are now inside Czechoslovakia," they said, "most likely heading toward the Carpathian Mountains" also known as the Tátra Mountains. This indicated that we were heading towards the Polish border — a very bad omen indeed.

Only now do I comprehend the total bewilderment and torment that my dear father and mother must have felt during those five weeks in the Ghetto and especially in the cattle boxcar deportation train. They were unable to verbalize their deep fear and concern for their children, and were helpless to try rescue us or even prepare us for the worst. Their agony and trepidation was multiplied by their inability to predict what lay ahead.

The situation was clearly beyond our parents' accumulated life experience, knowledge or imagination. They had no way of dealing with this terrible situation which engulfed the Jewish people and their own family in particular.

Mostly, they were quiet. They appeared severely disoriented and traumatized. We could see them deeply lost in their helpless agony. They looked pale, sad, haunted and tormented. They hardly spoke a word to each other or to us.

With the long sidetracked stops along the way, it took us about three to four days to reach Auschwitz-Birkenau. Throughout this time, our captors gave us no food. We carefully nibbled and shared with others the few morsels we had from home. There was barely enough to sustain life.

Darkest days on the calendar

* April 16, 1944: The Hungarian Government announced that all Jews in the Vásárosnamény area were to be transferred into Ghettos.

April 1944

Sunday	Monday	Tuesday	Wednesday	Thursday	Friday	Saturday
						8 Nisan 5704 Tzav Shabbat ha-Gadol **1**
9 Nisan 5704 **2**	10 Nisan 5704 **3**	11 Nisan 5704 **4**	12 Nisan 5704 **5**	13 Nisan 5704 **6**	14 Nisan 5704 **7**	15 Nisan 5704 Mishchu 1 Pesach. **8**
16 Nisan 5704 2 Pesach. **9**	17 Nisan 5704 1 Chol ha-Moed Pesach. **10**	18 Nisan 5704 2 Chol ha-Moed Pesach. **11**	19 Nisan 5704 3 Chol ha-Moed Pesach. **12**	20 Nisan 5704 4 Chol ha-Moed Pesach. **13**	21 Nisan 5704 7 Pesach. **14**	22 Nisan 5704 Aser Te'aser 8 Pesach. **15**
23 Nisan 5704 **16**	24 Nisan 5704 **17**	25 Nisan 5704 **18**	26 Nisan 5704 **19**	27 Nisan 5704 **20**	28 Nisan 5704 **21**	29 Nisan 5704 Shemini **22**
30 Nisan 5704 Rosh-Chodesh. **23**	1 Iyyar 5704 Rosh-Chodesh. **24**	2 Iyyar 5704 **25**	3 Iyyar 5704 **26**	4 Iyyar 5704 **27**	5 Iyyar 5704 **28**	6 Iyyar 5704 Tazri'a Metzora **29**
7 Iyyar 5704 **30**						

May 1944

Sunday	Monday	Tuesday	Wednesday	Thursday	Friday	Saturday
	8 Iyyar 5704 **1**	9 Iyyar 5704 **2**	10 Iyyar 5704 **3**	11 Iyyar 5704 **4**	12 Iyyar 5704 **5**	13 Iyyar 5704 Acharei Mot Kedoshim **6**
14 Iyyar 5704 Pesach-Shaini. **7**	15 Iyyar 5704 **8**	16 Iyyar 5704 **9**	17 Iyyar 5704 **10**	18 Iyyar 5704 Lag ba-Omer. **11**	19 Iyyar 5704 **12**	20 Iyyar 5704 Emor **13**
21 Iyyar 5704 **14**	22 Iyyar 5704 **15**	23 Iyyar 5704 **16**	24 Iyyar 5704 **17**	25 Iyyar 5704 **18**	26 Iyyar 5704 **19**	27 Iyyar 5704 Be-Har Be-Chukkotai **20**
28 Iyyar 5704 **21**	29 Iyyar 5704 **22**	1 Sivan 5704 Rosh-Chodesh. **23**	2 Sivan 5704 **24**	3 Sivan 5704 **25**	4 Sivan 5704 **26**	5 Sivan 5704 Be-Midbar **27**
6 Sivan 5704 1 Shavuot. **28**	7 Sivan 5704 2 Shavuot. **29**	8 Sivan 5704 **30**	9 Sivan 5704 **31**			

June 1944

Sunday	Monday	Tuesday	Wednesday	Thursday	Friday	Saturday
				10 Sivan 5704 **1**	11 Sivan 5704 **2**	12 Sivan 5704 Naso **3**
13 Sivan 5704 **4**	14 Sivan 5704 **5**	15 Sivan 5704 **6**	16 Sivan 5704 **7**	17 Sivan 5704 **8**	18 Sivan 5704 **9**	19 Sivan 5704 Be-Ha'alotcha **10**
20 Sivan 5704 **11**	21 Sivan 5704 **12**	22 Sivan 5704 **13**	23 Sivan 5704 **14**	24 Sivan 5704 **15**	25 Sivan 5704 **16**	26 Sivan 5704 Shelach **17**
27 Sivan 5704 **18**	28 Sivan 5704 **19**	29 Sivan 5704 **20**	30 Sivan 5704 Rosh-Chodesh. **21**	1 Tammuz 5704 Rosh-Chodesh. **22**	2 Tammuz 5704 **23**	3 Tammuz 5704 Korach **24**
4 Tammuz 5704 **25**	5 Tammuz 5704 **26**	6 Tammuz 5704 **27**	7 Tammuz 5704 **28**	8 Tammuz 5704 **29**	9 Tammuz 5704 **30**	

* April 17 or 18, 1944: The Hungarian gendarmes forced us into the Ghetto in Beregszász.
* April 17 or 18 to May 21 or 22, 1944: The five weeks that we spent in the open brick factory yard, which became known as the Ghetto of Beregszász.
* May 21 or 22, 1944: The Hungarian gendarmes aimed their loaded guns at us and forced us into cattle boxcar trains for our 3-4 day trip to Auschwitz-Birkenau.
* May 24, 1944: The last cattle boxcar train transport left the Beregszász Ghetto for Auschwitz-Birkenau.
* Thursday, May 25, 1944: We arrived at Birkenau-Auschwitz. On the Jewish calendar, the date was the 3rd of Sivan. The Germans murdered my father and my younger brother Sholem Yosef on the day of our arrival, just as they did with the many thousands of cattle box-car-loads of people who arrived before and after us. *We commemorate the Yahrtzeit (date of death) of my father and younger brother Sholem Yosef on the 3rd day of Sivan.*
* June 14, 1944 (23rd day of Sivan) — The Germans mur-dered my mother and oldest sister, Gizi (Gittel). *We commemorate the Yahrtzeit (date of death) of my mother and older sister Gittel on the 23rd day of Sivan.*

❄ **3** ❄

Auschwitz-Birkenau

Arrival...

On May 25, 1944, at about 9:00 in the morning, our cattle train lurched slowly and heavily back and forth a number of times. We then heard tense screeching of steel wheels, railroad whistles, bell clanging sounds, and the train abruptly stopped. We had arrived in Auschwitz-Birkenau* (Oswiecim & Brezinka in Polish, and Oshpitsin in Yiddish).

After a short and anxious interval, the heavy sliding-doors were pushed open from the outside, and suddenly we saw daylight again. The men who opened the doors appeared to be in their early 20's. They wore strange-looking, striped, blue-gray pajama-like pants and jackets, and on their heads they had round, striped, "sailor" caps that matched their thin pajama clothes.

Once the door was open, they shouted at us in Yiddish, again and again, that we must get out of the boxcar at once and leave everything in the train. They repeatedly yelled that our belongings would be brought to our living quarters.

During the following days, I sadly learned that this was a standard lie the SS ordered them to tell all new arrivals. Of course, we had no way of knowing this at the time.

It was a bright and sunny morning and the blue May sky was exceptionally clear. The youngsters jumped off the three-foot-high boxcars, but there were no steps or ramps for

---

* The Auschwitz-Birkenau Concentration Camps complex consisted of three main camps, with 45 sub-camps within a 50-60 kilometer radius.

the others. So we proceeded to help the elderly, the women, the old and wounded veterans, the smaller children, nursing mothers and the infirm, who were clearly in no position to jump down onto the platform. Slowly, with our help, they all stumbled out. The fresh morning air felt warm and pleasing to our tired bodies, as did our ability to turn freely in all directions and stretch our backs and limbs in the warmth of the gleaming sun.

Ever so mindful of the armed Nazi SS* surrounding us, we had little choice but to follow quietly and obediently the orders they barked at us in German. We managed to understand a fair number of these orders because the German language sounded so similar to the Yiddish we often spoke at home.

We were physically exhausted, hungry and thirsty. We were in a state of mental shock and fear, not knowing where we were or what was about to happen to us. We were really in various stages of emotional numbness. Having had little sleep and food over the previous days, most of us dragged our feet like zombies.

Adding to our confusion, some 300/400 feet ahead of us, we saw a tall wrought-iron ornamental sign proclaiming a terse German sentence, "ARBEIT MACHT FREI" (WORK MAKES YOU FREE). It was clearly not a temporary sign, since both ends were firmly anchored in the ground. It seemed to be a permanent welcoming sign and symbol, intended to astonish visitors and confuse new arrivals.

To further enhance the surrealism of our situation, flanking both sides of the large sign were rows of 4 or 5 musicians. They all wore what appeared to be fair-quality, multicolored business jackets and pants. Some stood and some sat on an assortment of old kitchen and dining room chairs, playing a medley of strikingly soothing and pleasing melodies. With a complete range of large and small musical instruments, they

---

* There were a number of SS groups: the Schutzstaffel SS, the Waffen SS, the Allgemeine SS, and others.

appeared to be a small orchestra, playing in welcome of our arrival. Several large pots of colorful spring flowers had been placed nearby.

The scene was eerie. My impression upon disembarking from the boxcars was of a large, overcrowded marketplace, jam-packed with civilian-clothed people and children, pushing and shoving forward at the commands of the shouting SS guards.

But this was no marketplace. We were captives inside a Nazi prison, with SS guards holding mad dogs on leashes.

We certainly were not aware of it at that time, but we had arrived at the "Gates of Hell."

About 15 minutes after our arrival, while carrying our personal belongings away, one of the pajama-clad inmates cautiously mumbled in Yiddish, *"Dos is Auschwitz-Birkenau!"* Giving no further explanation, he rushed-by without making eye contact, and soon disappeared from sight with two suitcases in his hands. However, the words "Auschwitz-Birkenau" held no meaning for me. I was still unaware that we had arrived at the murder center of the world.

Even at this point, we could not imagine that the Germans were setting us up for gassing and mass murder. In fact, about 20 minutes after we emerged from the train, while my family was still together, Father's emergency plan was; "As soon as we get through with this, write to Szécsy Károly in Tiszakerecseny, and make sure you come home. We will meet at home. Don't go anywhere else. Just go to Vásárosnamény and let us wait for each other at home."

It is quite obvious from these nearly last words of his, that he did not comprehend the gravity of the situation.

Families are separated

Suddenly, I saw a few hundred feet further up the line that it was splitting into several columns. I had no way of understanding or interpreting this separation of families. The people went like blind, innocent lambs to slaughter. By this time, most of us were shuffling with numbed feet, standing in line with drooping and bleary eyes. We were way beyond the ability to consider not complying with the shouted orders to *Line up!*, and *Move Forward!* The furious screaming sounds and the atmosphere of reigning terror are hard to describe.

When I looked at the ominous setting, I instantly understood that any commotion, disturbance or opposition to the German commands would be fraught with danger, and very likely lead to immediate harm to all of us. I was thinking especially of my parents and siblings. I felt instinctively that our best hope for survival was by remaining quiet and obeying the orders shouted at us. We were like hostages, totally overwhelmed by our captors' organization, planning, weaponry and ferocious dogs. And we were exhausted, alone, and devoid of everything, except the hope to survive.

The pushing and shoving in the various lineups continued unabated, as the SS men kept up the pressure with their mean-looking, barking and snarling German shepherds, their threats and screams. Undoubtedly, they did all this in order to keep us from talking and organizing. The combination of pressure and terror in this confusing, alien place was designed to keep everyone bewildered, stunned and on their best behavior.

To add to the terror, the Nazis' vicious German Shepherds were snarling and threatening those standing near them, and in turn our people pushed each other relentlessly, hoping to avoid the dogs' reach. Thus, the SS created a tightly formed line in which we were continuously pushing each other.

I guess that Táttee and Mommy were not aware of the extreme gravity of the situation, nor could they have understood the true reasons for the separation of families — of women from men, of young from old. By this time, we could plainly see families being separated only a short distance ahead of us. If our parents were aware of what it all meant, they certainly did not tell us.

The next barked SS order shouted into our face forbade us from talking. We therefore limited ourselves to whispering short sentences to siblings and parents, without turning our heads or making eye contact.

The SS continued to shout orders at us, as families ahead of us lined up with young children hanging on to their mothers' skirts, and parents holding their babies in their weary arms. The SS constantly shouted, *Mach Schnell! Mach Schnell!* (Make it Fast! Hurry Up!) With a wave of their hands, they motioned us to the left or right, casually yet fatefully separating family members from each other. This continued without us understanding or knowing the reason for the separation.

I tried hard to understand the anxious look in the eyes of my parents, siblings and adults around me, but I did not succeed. At one point, I suddenly saw my mother trying to hide her face as she wiped tears from her eyes. Even now, the pain is still there, and I find it difficult to communicate these memories. These are moments I definitely do not wish to remember. Nevertheless, I must write this now, so future generations will know and forever remember.

Standing there in those first hours in Auschwitz, as a youngster of 16½, I had no way of realizing that I was seeing the faces of my parents and four of my siblings for the very last time. (Although I did see Baruch one more time in Auschwitz for a few minutes.)

Minutes later, the SS murderers ordered our women to form their own line and to separate themselves from the men. With this command, Mommy, Gizi, Ruci, and Bina Rivka were separated from us. A bit further on, Mommy and Gizi were separated from Ruci and Bina Rivka. However, it turned out that the gassing showers and crematoria lacked the capacity to massacre the vast number of people who arrived that day from the numerous Hungarian ghettos. Therefore, the Germans "stored" the overflow of victims in nearby containment blocks. My mother and sister Gizi were among those "stored" for later annihilation.

About ten minutes later, the men reached the SS 'selection' line. My father and younger brother Sholem Yosef were motioned to separate themselves from my older brother, Baruch, and me. Within minutes, they disappeared from sight. I did not realize that this was the last time we were ever to see each other.

Suddenly, there was some shifting of the pushing lines and my brother Baruch disappeared from view. I found myself all alone and lost track of my entire family. There I was, a youngster of 16½, without a clue as to where my family had disappeared.

Events were happening quickly and furiously. I was numb and confused. I was unable to understand what was happening, and there was no one to ask. What's more, talking was forbidden; *"sprechen ist verboten,"* the SS kept shouting angrily.

From the looks on their faces, the people in front and behind me seemed just as scared and bewildered as I was. Like some kind of robot, I just moved on and followed the men in front of me. There seemed to be no end to the horror and terror.

On the very day of arrival, I found myself separated from everybody in my family, without saying a goodbye to any one of them. But at that time I still did not know that THIS SEPARATION WAS FOREVER. *We were robbed even of the chance to say goodbye.*

I later learned that this was the infamous, dreaded "selection line," supervised and often conducted by the white-gloved German devil, Dr. Josef Mengele.

Sometime during the next half hour, I became aware that my line had melted into another line to our right. Suddenly, to my surprise, I found myself in front of a young man at a small, decrepit card table, wearing the grey-blue striped pajama uniform. On his table was a quart-sized wine bottle, half-full with a bluish liquid that looked like ink. In his undersized hand appeared to be an odd-looking needle on a short stick, something like a peculiar fountain pen. His assistant at the table ordered me to stick out my left arm and he held it tightly. Before I was fully aware of what he was doing, my arm had been tattooed. With that act, on that very afternoon, I lost my name, and became a number. The dark blue number tattoo I received was "A.9561."

From the tattooing table, I was motioned to join another line where another striped-clothed man gave me a prisoner's haircut. Within two minutes, I was relieved of all my hair.

Soon thereafter, someone ordered our group of about 120 to 150 selected youngish men to undress on the street and drop all our clothes and shoes onto large piles. They had us walk away stark naked from the area and onto a nearby smaller path.

About 100 feet past our pile of clothing was yet another pajama-clad inmate, standing with a bucket of kerosene. He soaked his rag with kerosene and wetted my bare head and chest and soaked my exposed underarms and private parts. The kerosene oozed into my eyes and ears, but as I tried to wipe it away, my bare hands only managed to push the liquid further into my eyes, burning it even more.

I had now become a disinfected, dehumanized being. I felt that I had suffered the utter destruction of my basic human dignity, indeed...of my very humanity.

About an hour or two later, as we were still standing stark naked on some open street, the SS herded us another 500 feet down the road into an open shower room for a fast cold shower. We received no towels and stood naked outside the shower room for about an hour, while the water evaporated off our bare skin and our bald heads. Finally, men wearing the strange striped pajamas, handed us the same uniform they themselves wore: striped pants, a round striped cap, a striped jacket, and someone else's shoes. We were given neither underwear nor socks.

At this point I realized that I had been stripped of all my earthly possessions. I had no underwear, no undershirt, no shirt, no socks, no handkerchief, no knife, no pencil, no paper, no comb, no identification document, and of course, no money.

To further demoralize and weaken us physically and mentally, the SS did not let us have any water to drink, nor food to eat all day. The leftover food, which we had so carefully saved up and rationed during the cattle boxcar train ride, was in our packs and suitcases, which they had not allowed us to take. I had not eaten a bite since very early that morning and I was hungry and worse — very thirsty.

The pajama-clad prisoners had told us that morning that they would bring our belongings to our living quarters. They lied. In hindsight, it is obvious that this was just another devious ruse of the SS, designed to keep us calm while they separated us from our families and belongings. The Germans were exceptionally well-organized, and they seemed to know very well how to run the world's most methodical and diabolical mass-murder factory.

It was slowly getting dark, and the sun was beginning to disappear when they finally ordered our group to line up five abreast. By this time, we were mere exhausted animals, barely shuffling our feet, hardly able to feel or think.

After a 20-minute march on a dark road, the guards with their dogs herded our group into one of several big barracks, where someone pointed me to the third tier of a bare wooden bunk bed. It had nothing at all on it — not even a bit of straw. Like everyone else, I climbed up and lay down, wearing the striped clothes I had received earlier. There were seven tired, exhausted men next to me, all sharing this bunk.

Weary, thirsty, hungry, exhausted and completely drained,

I fell asleep on that crudely constructed bunkbed — a raw plank of wood.

Zehl Appell: Daily physical and mental abuse

Early the next morning, I awoke to a tremendous noise. A sudden outburst of shouting and cursing in the German language blasted the air. Numerous angry-looking men were hastily pacing among the rows of bunk beds and blowing powerful ear-piercing whistles, without stop. Their shrieks of *Zehl Appell!* (Roll Call!), *Rauss! Rauss!* (Out! Out!), *Faule Hund!* (Lazy Dogs!) and *Shmutzige Schwein!* (Dirty Pigs!) pierced my jittery ears. While I was yet unable to translate the words into my native Hungarian or Yiddish, I certainly sensed the intent of the furiously shouted orders.

The first order of the day was to rush outside and line up like soldiers, five men to a row. All of us lined up and stood at attention. Additional commands were no talking, no whispering and no movement of any kind. Terror reigned. Known as the *Zehl Appell*, this was the dreaded and often deadly roll call. During the one to two hours of standing at full "attention," the *Stubedienst* (Room servant), the *Blockaeltester* (Block-elder) and the SS counted us repeatedly. Finally, they dismissed us and sent us back into the block,* ordering everyone immediately back into his assigned perch in the empty bunk bed.

The *Blockaeltester*, who was also a prisoner, was the man in charge — the boss of everything that went on inside the block and during the *Zehl Appell*. He could do anything he wanted to a *haftling* (prisoner), including beat him to death, and no one but the SS could question his actions. Of course,

---

* "Block" usually refers to a larger building containing from 200 to 1000 men or women in one building. "Barrack" usually refers to a one story barn-like building containing from 100 to 300 men or women.

the SS generally showed no interest in questioning his judgment, especially regarding beatings of *haftlinge* (prisoners) who were mostly Jews.*

The *Zehl Appell* harassment was repeated twice daily. The act of standing at attention in one spot for extended periods caused some men to faint and led to health problems for many others. No emergency latrine visits were ever allowed during these "all-important" *Zehl Appell* sessions.

It seems that the main purpose of these drawn-out, torturous counting procedures was to intimidate, degrade and injure us both physically and emotionally. Severe beatings were meted out for such "crimes" as not standing straight enough during *Zehl Appell*, for sneezing, helping ease the pain of a man standing next to you, turning the head to observe maltreatment or a cry, or even wiping a wounded eye.

The guards pulled out of the *Zehl Appell* line anyone who appeared to be weak, had leg cramps after standing in one place for so long, or just did not look fit in the eyes of the Germans. Of course, being pulled out meant a one-way trip to the gas chamber and the crematorium. On occasion, during a particularly tough *Zehl Appell* session, the thought that "this could be it for me" passed through all of our minds.

We became like sleepwalkers, automatons set to react to expletives and their shouted commands. We wanted to run like a rabbit or hide like a rat, but there was nowhere to go and nowhere to hide. Brutality was the daily way of life. Every day, they created new horrors — horrors that only the highly-educated, well-trained, white-gloved German people were capable of creating. This routine was a part of the systematic terror of Auschwitz-Birkenau.

About an hour after the *Zehl Appell* was over that first day,

---

* And yes, there were exceptions to all rules.

they gave us some black coffee-like liquid and a small portion of black bread. This was our breakfast. It was the first food and liquid in my mouth since I was ordered off the cattle boxcar the previous morning.

This was our typical morning routine, the cruel start of each and every day in Auschwitz-Birkenau. Beyond the great hunger, our daily concern was to avoid the next beating from the dreaded Gestapo SS and the growling and biting from their snarling German shepherd dogs walking around us.

About five days later, I saw my brother Baruch walking on the other side of a six-foot-high, non-electric wire fence. It was a shocking and heartbreaking surprise to see him in the *haftling* uniform, and yet gratifying to see him alive. He saw me as well. Excitedly, we waved and approached the wire fence separating us. He told me he had seen two of our sisters, Ruci and Binah Rivka, a few days before. He also told me that the girls were close by, somewhere in one of the many women's heftlinge blocks. He was walking alongside his assigned horse-drawn wagon, delivering potatoes to the central kitchen inside the camp. Another kitchen he worked at, also in Auschwitz-Birkenau, was where meals were prepared for the Gestapo and SS Nazi guards.

We started to speak a few more words, until someone with a wooden stick threatened to beat him up for talking to me, so he ran back to his horse and wagon. To my deep sorrow, that was the last time we ever laid eyes on each other. Baruch did not survive the Holocaust.

The days passed very slowly. My mind was restless and incessantly occupied with somber thoughts about my parents, siblings, home life, friends, water and food. At night, on the bare wooden bunk, I tried to comfort myself and listen to some distant, mental noises I conjured up from my short, youthful life in Vásárosnamény, but there was nothing but the silence of my deep loneliness. I sorely missed having my parents' advice as to what to do.

About a week after my arrival in Auschwitz-Birkenau, I overheard grownup *heftlinge* whispering that there were a number of gas chambers and crematoria in this area of the camp where the Germans first gas and choke people to death and then burn them to ashes.

It dawned on me that this explained the unusual and strong smell I so often smelled in the air, especially under certain wind conditions.

Nevertheless, many of us simply refused to believe or entertain such horrible thoughts. I guess this was one form of "living in denial." We simply did not want to hear or believe these ideas.

Such was life in a German-invented, modern, industrialized, mass extermination and murder concentration-camp system.

After receiving a number of excruciating beatings on my head, ears, shoulders, arms and back, and after observing the bruised men around me, I somehow discovered that one of the secrets to survival in this criminal world was to become, as much as possible, *invisible*.

I learned eleven rules of survival in Auschwitz-Birkenau — do not ask any questions, do not act smart, do not talk back, do not volunteer, do not be late, and do not be early; if they tell you to stand, you stand; if they tell you to jump, you jump; if they tell you to sit, you sit; if you want to make it through this minute, this hour, or this day, then do not draw attention to yourself for any reason; moreover, never, ever ask why — just do it!

The verbal and physical abuse in the camp was constant, both inside and outside the Block. From any and every point of view, the conditions for inmates were abysmal. I slowly began to understand that the Germans had somehow received the world's approval to condemn us to slavery culminating in death or to instant death at the hands of Hitler's eager volunteer executioners. Yes, all SS men and women were strictly volunteers! But I still did not, and could not understand their voracious appetite for such extreme brutality.

A day in the Jaworzno Concentration Camp

Around June 12, 1944, perhaps two and a half weeks after my arrival in Auschwitz, some 35-40 inmates, including myself, were abruptly ordered by well-armed Gestapo or SS men to climb onto an unmarked, green flatbed truck. There were no benches on the truck. It had only four-foot-high sideboards and a removable backboard.

The Gestapo or SS men carried long guns on their shoulders, with pistols and pouches with spare bullets on their belts. They said nothing to us, but merely gestured in dismissal as one would to a dumb animal. As far as the SS were concerned, we were worth much less than animals.

They jammed us onto the truck until we were a solid standing mass. We had no idea where they were taking us, what they wanted of us, or what was about to happen to us. The SS driver took his time driving.

After about an hour on the highway, we found ourselves at the gate of a securely fortified concentration camp, which we later found out was named Jaworzno, also the name of a nearby Polish village. Upon our arrival, the receiving uniformed SS counted us twice. From the corner of my eye, I observed that someone from the receiving group signed various documents and handed them back to the truck driver, who also wore the SS uniform.

They had us stand at attention for about an hour and then herded us into one of the single-story wooden barracks that lined the perimeter of the camp. According to some of the early rumors we had heard, the Jaworzno Concentration Camp was one of the smaller satellite camps of the giant Auschwitz-Birkenau camp system. It held about 3,500 male captives.

A line of reinforced concrete posts that were about 10-12 feet high and curved inward at the top supported the inner barbed-wire fence, which surrounded the camp on all sides. The tall concrete posts were about 60 feet apart. About 18 feet outside the first line of barbed-wire fence was a second barbed-wire fence, identical in every way to the first. High watchtowers were strategically located between these two lines of fences, each with its own visible gun-turret. One, and sometimes two, uniformed SS soldiers were observable in each tower. When they changed shifts, we clearly saw them marching with bayonet-mounted rifles, and most of the time they were accompanied by German Shepherd dogs.

While all Jaworzno armed guards always wore the German SS uniforms, we heard many of them speaking German with heavy Ukrainian, Polish, or other accents. Actually they were non-Germans who had volunteered for the murderous "SS *Einsatzgruppen*" (Special Task and Action Units). The full German name was *Einsatzgruppen der Sicherheitsdienstes und der Sicherheitspolizei* (SIPO), loosely meaning "German Security Action Police Groups."

To discourage *Heftling* escape attempts, our *Blockaeltester* repeatedly warned us that these barbed wires were electrified. He pointed to the large metal signs posted on the fence, every 80 feet or so, which read: "Warning high voltage!" in German.

The majority of the Jaworzno *heftling* population consisted of Jews from Poland, Hungary, Czechoslovakia, Romania, Germany, Belgium, Ukraine, Russia, Yugoslavia, Greece and France. However, there was also a small number of captured American, Russian, British and other Allied soldiers, whose captivity in Jaworzno was in violation of the Geneva Convention, which Germany had signed, but summarily ignored.

Along with these Allied Army captives, there were some political prisoners from Germany and German-occupied countries, including Communists, trade unionists, Socialists, Jehovah's Witnesses and what the Germans called "undesirables," such as homosexuals, Gypsies and Seventh Day Adventists. In total, non-Jews comprised some 12-16% of the *heftlinge* population.

The Jaworzno Camp — which was actually a camp for forced slave-labor inmates — was run by the SS for the German I.G. Farben company.

Emotional support:
Hersh Baer Schwartz

My former neighbor and playmate, Hersh Baer (Tzvi Dov) Schwartz was on the same flatbed truck that transported me from Auschwitz to Jaworzno. We were happy but restrained, as we recognized each other, when we got off of the truck, in spite of the blue-gray concentration camp uniforms the Germans made us wear. We managed to stay together in the same barracks and also in our daily work assignment. It was a fortunate break, which benefited both of us. We had both been forcibly separated from our families and were all alone. We helped sustain each other in our dream of returning home, and reuniting with our families and resuming our former lives.

As far as we knew, Hersh Baer was the only one from his family, and I was the only one from my family there. There was really no way we could know this for sure. Visiting other barracks was a major crime, and prisoner lists were obviously not available to any *haftling*. Even the SS could not know for sure, as they knew us only by our tattooed numbers. They had purposely reduced us to mere numbers and had no record of our first and last names. It was a rare occurrence when a family member recognized another, either during a work assignment or by having been coincidentally assigned to the same barracks.

My life-sustaining partner, Hersh Baer (Béla) Schwartz
After liberation, 1946/1947

With no one else but each other, my friendship with Hersh Baer provided both of us with support and a sense of security, belonging, hope, and most of all, a renewed incentive to continue the ongoing difficult daily struggle to live. We slept on bunkbeds near each other, and looked out for each other all the time. In Jaworzno, we became surrogate family.

Although he was a bit younger than I, we had been boyhood friends — playmates and neighbors in our hometown, Vásárosnamény. As youngsters, our group of friends had spent many long, happy summer days climbing the plum and apple trees in his backyard or playing hide and seek, swinging on our swing and building castles in the white sand pile in our bakery yard.

Occasionally, we would pick up our friends and hike to his father's whiskey brewery at the northwestern end of town. The Schwartz brewery had several dozen huge wooden vats in which plums and other multi-colored fruits fermented slowly during the long summer and autumn.

Amidst the hell of Jaworzno, the two of us sometimes recalled the fun we had in his family brewery yard, observing that huge, pungent mass of fermenting "fruit-mash" turn into a steady trickle of clear, fruity, and rather costly alcohol. The grownups considered the transformed product delicious "Slivovitz" (plum brandy). Additionally, they made pear, apricot and apple whiskey. The brewery also provided us with an excellent place to play hide-and-seek games.

Our somewhat childlike reflections and memories of "last year" helped us sustain our sinking self-confidence and aided us in waging the daily struggle to survive. We whispered these hometown recollections to each other until we collapsed in our hard, bare bunk beds for the night.

We became like true twins throughout the Jaworzno nightmare, until the SS took Hersh Baer away on that terrible winter "Death-March" in January of 1945 — which he somehow survived.

Building a German electric generating plant

The town of Jaworzno is located in southern Poland, about 32 kilometers from Auschwitz-Birkenau and about 55 kilometers from the city of Krakow, then the capital city of Poland.

In 1944, Jaworzno was a small town, in a huge, historically-disputed land area. The Poles considered this region a part of Greater Poland, while expansionist Germany claimed the area as part of its *"Ober Schlesien"* (Upper Silesia). After Germany conquered Poland in 1939, they annexed the area and made it part of its expanding *Großdeutschland*, "Greater Germany."

The day after my arrival in Jaworzno, I was assigned to work for a subdivision of the I.G. Farben AG, a construction company hired to build the concrete structures and other items of a new coal-heated, steam-to-electricity power plant.

At the expense of Jewish blood and unimaginable suffering and death, the German Reich set out to develop this disputed coal-mining region for their *"Fatherland."* We were, in fact, building the new Wilhelm Electric Power Supply Company, known in German as the *Energie Versorgung Oberschlesien, A.G.* (Energy Supply Upper Silesia Corporation). This plant was to supply electric power for this growing region of their forcibly-acquired *Ober Schlesien* territory.

As I understand it, we were actually working directly for the I.G. Farben Company, a major German industrial and construction firm. It is still a powerful German corporation. (The latest information available is that they broke up into many corporations; most did extremely well, while others did not).

The Jaworzno slaves worked directly under the supervision of I.G. Farben engineers. I.G.Farben was a giant chemical, construction, and armaments conglomerate, which built the Auschwitz-Birkenau extermination gas-chambers and many of its slave-labor satellite camps. It is widely believed that without I.G. Farben's effort, Hitler would have had difficulty getting his war machine moving.*

All of the *heftlinge*, as well as the civilian engineers who guided us, worked for I.G. Farben Company. The engineers guided us on product quality matters and on technical details.

Interestingly, a company owned by Albert Speer owned the electric plant we were building, and Albert Speer just "happened" to be the Minister of Armaments for Germany, as well as Hitler's favorite architect during World War II.

The SS, in cooperation with the German government, supplied German industries with our toil and cheap slave labor, which we in Jaworzno and other Auschwitz-Birkenau satellite camps were forced to do. (It is my assumption that the SS charged a favorable labor fee to the I.G. Farben and Albert Speer companies).

Among the several coal mines in the area, the two important ones were the Friedrichsgrube and the Carlsgrube coal mines. The presence of these productive mines was probably the main reason the electric plant was built nearby. These mines were extensive and easily able to supply the coal needed to serve the new, steam-heated, electricity-generating plant for many years.

---

* *Hell's Cartel*, by Diarmuid Jeffreys, Metropolitan Books, 2008.

Slave-working in concrete
for I. G. Farben

I was assigned to work in the concrete-products manufacturing sub-group, which was building the Jaworzno power plant. For several days in a row, we worked unloading bags of cement from a line of parked freight trains on the periphery of the plant. Each of us had to carry two bags of cement on our backs from the train into the cement sheds, located in the concrete mixing area. With our meager daily food supply, even one bag of cement was too much, and consequently, many of us stumbled and fell. In addition to bruises from the tumble, we also suffered vindictive beatings from the German supervisor for tearing the cement bags and spilling part of its precious content.

We next unloaded trainloads of steel rods, heavy steel and hardwood beam-forms, and additional tools and supplies. A few of our men were indeed lucky; they received wheelbarrows for this grueling job. Later on, smaller crews ran the wheelbarrows full of sand and stone under similar difficult conditions.

The second week, we were divided into three crews. One crew cleaned, brushed, oiled and assembled a required quantity of the weighty metal and wooden beam forms and placed an assortment of reinforcing steel rods in them.

Another crew mixed and tumbled the cement-sand-and-stone aggregate according to the prescribed production method. To this dry mixture the crew had to add warm water instead of the typical cold, and then sprinkled into the mixer the Germans' "secret formula" — a small bagful of a gray chemical additive. We used this special mixture for most of the concrete beams and in all of the hollow building blocks that we produced, working six days a week.

A third crew wheelbarrowed and poured the wet, warm cement into the prepared beam forms, filling them only 65% to 70%, since the gray chemical powder acted on the cement as yeast does to dough. About 20 minutes after we poured the cement, the concrete rose and gently overflowed the beam-forms.

This chemical mix created millions of small bubbles of entrapped gas in the cement, thus increasing the cement volume by a substantial 30-35 percent. This unique concrete-rising process saved the Germans hard-to-get, expensive cement.

After about 30 minutes, our crew carefully twist-leveled and finished the top of the risen raw cement into its various poured forms with spinning round steel rods. When the new beams set and were sufficiently dry, we cautiously disassembled the frames and carried the fresh cement beams into a large drying yard. Finally, we rushed back to clean, oil, and reassemble the beam forms for the next pouring of fresh cement for more beams.

The day-to-day work was backbreaking. The hours were long and the German supervisors pushed us hard all the time. I was indeed very lucky, because I was almost immediately assigned to a new and kind *Kapo* (an SS-appointed work-group supervisor usually for a large number of workers). *Kapo* Schteig was able and willing to take the risk of interceding on our behalf and he often got us better working conditions.

Generally, though not always, the *Kapos* and *Blockaeltesters* and their assistants were quite hard on us. They often acted that way in order to keep their special jobs and receive extra rations of food, and perhaps other privileges as well.

Each *Kapo* had to make his own decision as to how much he was ready to "pay" ... at our expense... in order to retain his privileged position.

There were four types of *Kapos* in charge of us:

1) Those who tried the job but soon gave it up because they would not — or could not — enforce the tough SS rules.

2) Those who thrived in the job, as it gave them an opportunity to vent their frustrations at their own incarceration and painful losses of their own families.

3) Those who were natural sadists and/or anti-Semites. They enjoyed the elevated status and pleasured in the pain they could inflict on helpless concentration camp inmates.

4) And finally, there were those like *Kapo* Schteig, a Jew, who helped the camp inmates by convincing the SS men in charge and the German civilian engineers that by easing the pressure on the slave-workers, they would save cement and get a better concrete building product.

Kapo Schteig: Angel of life

Schteig was from Munkács, (Mukachevo),* which is currently in southwestern Ukraine. I am not sure of his surname spelling, but his first name was Mordechay. At some stage in his younger years he had moved to Belgium and found work there. During the Hitler years, the Germans deported him together with all Jews of Belgium, and he became a *haftling* in Jaworzno.

Kapo Schteig was a tall, husky man and spoke a fluent German. His effortless use of the German language helped him to get along with the German engineers, the Gestapo and the SS management. Like all men in his position, he had to enforce the rules as dictated by the SS. However, he was willing to take the risks which were inherent in interceding on our behalf, and he certainly helped us in many ways.

He convinced the construction engineers to station additional workers to lift and carry the heavy, steel-reinforced concrete beams. He pointed out that there would be less stress and breakage in the newly-formed, moist concrete beams, as we carried them by hand from the manufacturing

---

* The only Hungarian town with a slight Jewish majority, until 1944 when all the Jews were deported to Auschwitz. Hungary acquired it in 1938 from Czechoslovakia, under whose control it had come in about 1920.

point to the drying area.

He also secured additional workers to help unload the heavy cement bags from the trains and got the Germans to agree that we should carry only one bag at a time, instead of the two bags we had had to carry the first week. *Kapo* Schteig reasoned with them that there would be less cement waste.

During the summer weeks, *Kapo* Schteig noted the need to sprinkle water on all the new concrete products to prevent the fresh beams from cracking. He also advised his superiors that the newly poured cement would turn out stronger if it dried slowly. This provided an easy job for 2 men, sprinkling water onto the new concrete during the hot summer days. I was very fortunate to have been one of the two sprinklers for a part of the summer of 1944.

He also convinced the engineers of the importance of a clean construction site, thus creating two relatively easy jobs for two floor cleaners and pack-away men.

At great personal risk, *Kapo* Schteig found unique ways to notify us of imminent inspections by the SS, the civilian-clothed German engineers and managers. When he saw SS men or the civilian managers starting to inspect our construction area, he would take a huge stick or branch and pretend to aggressively beat us with it. He banged it vigorously as he passed by the hollow walls of the storage sheds, trying to make as much noise as he possibly could. *Kapo* Schteig would also begin furiously cursing and shouting at us in German, demanding that we work faster and faster. Then, in a lower voice, he gave us the Hebrew signal, *"Geshem, Geshem"* (Rain, Rain), to indicate that the Germans were coming and that his shouting and cursing was only in order to save our necks and backs. His wild shouts and curses enabled us to save ourselves. During the months I worked under him, I never saw him hit anybody.

Typically, within minutes of his put-on show of disciplining us, the SS or the German civilian managers showed up for their nasty tour of inspection. The warnings from *Kapo* Schteig often saved our emaciated bodies. Had the Germans caught us pausing to wipe the sweat off our faces, using the latrine, or getting a drink of water, we would get a beating or other punishment from the German and Ukrainian SS men.

Furthermore, on the long walk to and from our job site, whenever *Kapo* Schteig saw anybody stumbling or in distress, he unobtrusively got someone to help. Many of us were young, inexperienced kids, in need of all the help we could get.

Kapo Schteig did have one problem that no other *Kapo* had. The SS had put him in charge of about 125 to 200 men. But many a morning at counting time, up to 15 extra men showed up, falsely claiming that they had been assigned to work under him.

Of course, the reason that *Kapo* Schteig had extra men in his lineup was that the inmates heard that he was a *"mentch"* (a decent person who treated his charges decently) and tried to get the Germans to give us better working conditions. Many *heftlinge* wanted to leave their dreadful workstations and tried their utmost to get work under the more lenient *Kapo* Schteig.

This presented a dangerous dilemma for him. The SS gave him a rough time for his inability to control the surplus workers, allotting him just a few minutes to set things straight — or else he would be beaten. He had to struggle many a morning to remove those extra men whom he believed had not been assigned to him. Understandably, those whom *Kapo* Schteig pulled from his lineup were very angry at him, but he really had no choice.

For many of us, *Kapo* Schteig represented a small sliver of a friendly rainbow in the large gloomy sky. He was a breath of fresh air in this putrid hell of abuse and murder. I can truly say that he saved my life many times.

Rabbi Friedman of Ráchev

It was several weeks after my arrival at Jaworzno and my assignment to the concrete products group, when I first met an
elderly man named Friedman. Subsequently, I heard by way of
whispers that he was the Rabbi Shlómo Zálman Friedman of
Rahó, known in *Yiddish* as the town of Ráchev. He was among
the recent arrivals to Jaworzno, from Auschwitz-Birkenau. He
was one of the few who looked relatively old in this work-to-
death concentration camp, yet somehow, he managed to pass
the daily age-and-appearance selections by the SS and succeeded in staying alive during the Auschwitz-Birkenau *Zehl
Appell* nightmares.

Two of his adult sons, Lippa, a family man before the war,
and Yitzchok, who appeared to be in his mid-twenties and single, were also there with him. However, they were located in
different barracks and had different work assignments. There
was not much visible contact between them, and none of them
was able to help the other. Visiting other barracks was a major
crime, and few people braved that risk.

Rabbi Friedman, like other men who once held leadership
positions, kept secret the fact that he had been a community
Rabbi. That sort of information invited additional beatings,
ridicule, and other abuse.

Within a short time, the *Rav* (Rabbi) reached a point where
he had no strength to keep up with the grueling pace. He
clearly needed help to survive the long and difficult daily
marches to and from the construction site. One can well imagine that his former rabbinic position left him physically and
mentally unprepared for the difficult physical work and daily
horrors of the Jaworzno Concentration Camp.

Kapo Schteig took him under his wing and asked his work
supervisor to find the *Rav* less taxing work. The next day, *Kapo*
Schteig asked Hersh Baer Schwartz and me to look after the
Rav. The two of us decided that we would each take the *Rav* by
an arm and help him walk to and from work. We kept him from

stumbling or falling out of line on the rough road, lest it invite a beating from the SS or nasty bites from their snarling watchdogs, which always accompanied the SS guards on the daily march.

This help was especially important for the *Rav* whenever the German or Ukrainian SS decided to give us a particularly hard time and forced us to jog or speed-walk part of the way to or from work. After a long day of hard work and abuse, many of us barely had the strength to march back to camp.

I heard from surviving friends that the SS shot and killed Rabbi Friedman's older son, Lippa, during the terrible winter evacuation, known as the "Death March," but the Rabbi and Yitzchok did survive. After liberation, Yitzchok went to Israel, where he owned a furniture store in Bnei Barak. Rabbi Friedman settled in Lugano, Switzerland where he served as Rav. He authored a Talmudic work titled *Zivchei Shlómo*. He passed away in 1980.

Purchasing Tefillin in Jaworzno?

An extraordinary episode happened one July evening in Jaworzno. A young man in his mid 20s, wearing the same striped *haftling* outfit as all the rest of us, approached Hersh Baer and me and started speaking a language that we did not understand. However, as we paid closer attention to his rapid speech and repeated words, we started to process what he was saying, and realized that he was speaking a classical Sephardi-accented Hebrew. Though we were not familiar with the sound of the accented Ivrit as he pronounced it, we slowly began to understand him.

It turned out that he was Jewish, an aviator, and a Greek citizen. He had been serving with the Allied Air Forces, and his plane had been shot down over German-occupied France. The Germans captured him after he bailed out of his damaged airplane. In accordance with the criminal norms of Germany, the

Nazis dumped him in the Jaworzno concentration camp, complete with his backpack of personal belongings and his pair of *Tefillin*.

By accepted international law and according to the Geneva Convention, all military captives were supposed to be placed in a prisoner-of-war (POW) camp, and accorded certain basic rights. They were certainly not to be incarcerated in a concentration-extermination camp. The Germans habitually violated the international Geneva Convention rules, which they had solemnly signed and agreed to abide by. They frequently sent captured Allied soldiers to concentration camps and forced them to work for the German Fatherland. In short, they simply worked these POWs to death.

As previously mentioned, the Germans took away all our possessions when we arrived at Auschwitz-Birkenau. We were left with no personal effects at all, not even a handkerchief. Upon arrival in Jaworzno, the SS gave me a rusty metal bowl for soup, a metal coffee cup without a handle, and a four-inch-long steel soup spoon. These were my only earthly possessions in Jaworzno.

However, this Greek Jewish aviator was lucky. He had been able to retain the personal possessions in his backpack. He was now trying to sell us some of them including his pair of *Tefillin*. Since we had no money, we had to barter in food. We finally struck a deal, whereby every second day we would give him one portion of our soup, until we had given him seven days worth of soup. On those days when we gave him a portion of soup, Hersh Baer and I each ate only half of one portion of soup. This extra burden of reduced food was quite hard on us, and even dangerous for our survival, but we were young and foolish.

On our long walk to work, we managed to quietly tell the Rachev'er Rav about our secret *Tefillin* purchase. We told him that for the last week, the two of us had been stealthily putting on *Tefillin* early each morning and saying the *Shma Yisrael* and

Shmoneh Esrei prayers as we remembered them by heart. The *Tefillin* became our daily connection to G-d and a tangible tie to our families. The *Tefillin* also offered us solace and memories of our former daily practice at home.

We offered the Rav daily use of our *Tefillin* during the short break, between awakening in the morning and standing in the tormenting *Zehl Appell* roll-call line. He suggested that we say only the *Bráchot* (benedictions over the *Tefillin*) and if there was enough time, the first part of *Shma Yisrael*. The rest of *Shma* and *Shmoneh Esrei* should be left for afterwards. This way we would be able to share the *Tefillin* not only with him, but also with about six other trusted neighbors, who would sneak into our bunk area and quickly, very briefly don the *Tefillin*. We soon followed his advice.

Being young and hasty, we did not think of the possibility that sharing our *Tefillin* with others would increase the likelihood of being caught in the act of putting them on. We also did not realize that in addition to our hunger pains from the lost portions of soups, we had also created a constant problem: the daily quandary of how and where to hide the *Tefillin*. If we were found with the *Tefillin*, not only would we lose them, but we might also be punished, even killed, for such a major infraction of the rules. We prayed and hoped every day that no one would find our hidden secret.

As youngsters, we were unable to come to terms with the sad fact that we had by now forgotten parts of our daily prayers. After all, these were prayers that we had known by heart, saying them instinctively for years. I often blamed these mental blocks on our severe malnutrition, along with the daily physical and mental strain. Luckily, Rabbi Friedman helped us out of such mental blocks.

A few days before Yom Kippur of 1944, Rabbi Friedman was in the infirmary for a couple of days. *Kapo* Schteig had intervened on his behalf, and managed to make some excuse to get him a few days of rest. While in the infirmary, he sent a message through *Kapo* Shteig, and asked that we do him a big favor and sneak the *Tefillin* to him for use on the day before Yom Kippur. But we were reluctant to take that chance. We thought it was too risky to sneak the *Tefillin* to the infirmary, and then back again to our hiding place. This was just too much to ask, I reasoned.

Nevertheless, Hersh Baer worked out a deal with Rabbi Friedman, whereby in return for our extra risk, he would 'bless us' before Yom Kippur. As the holy day arrived, we actually felt good about this arrangement, because the custom in both our homes was that our fathers would bless us every Yom Kippur Eve, before going to synagogue.

We snuck up to his infirmary window and very gently tapped on it. He reached his hands out to touch our heads while he quietly whispered the traditional blessing *Yesimcha Elokim*, "May G-d make you like Ephraim and Menashe..." In the end, the *Tefillin* did get back safely to their hiding place in our barrack.

Hersh Baer managed to save them during the Death March out of Jaworzno in the winter of 1944. Although he subsequently lost them after the war, they offered us comfort and hope in our time of need.

I consider the *Tefillin* episode as one of the important and momentous chapters of my survival in the Jaworzno Concentration Camp.

Talmudic thoughts in Jaworzno

Under normal conditions, Sunday was our day off from slave-labors at the I.G. Farben electrical plant construction site. One hot summer Sunday evening in early August 1944, Hersh Baer and I observed four adults — Kapo Schteig, Rabbi Friedman, a Mr. Zeidenfeld from Munkács, and another man — standing in the shade of a nearby barrack, carrying on a spirited conversation. They seemed to be quite deep into their discussion and oblivious of the putrid world around them.

This was an extraordinary sight. Open assemblies of this nature were prohibited and usually invited a beating from the nearby *Blockaeltester* or one of the lesser *haftling* officials. Since we knew three of these four men, we became interested. The conversation piqued our curiosity, and we did not want to miss something important that might help our daily effort to survive. However, we dared not join them. After all, these four men were just about the oldest prisoners among us, while we, not yet 17, represented the youngest segment of the Jaworzno Concentration Camp population. We assumed that these older men would probably resent an intrusion.

We therefore turned our backs to them and slowly and inconspicuously drifted backwards, drawing closer and closer, while pretending to pay no attention to them or their conversation.

Once we were within earshot, we were surprised and elated to hear the four men animatedly reminiscing about their youthful years in their respective *yeshivot*. They were whisperingly going over, in *Yiddish*, a section of *Gemara* (Talmud) and the commentaries as best they could remember them.

Hersh Baer and I enjoyed eavesdropping on the murmured Talmudic conversation of these four mature *heftlinge* in such an unlikely, diabolical and irreverent place. For those 15 minutes, we felt as if we were drugged and transferred to some far away dream-island.

Wretched daily life

Jaworzno was an all-around hell. We went to bed with hunger pangs every night and woke up starved every morning. Beatings, hunger, physical threats, fear and uncertainty were omnipresent in our lives. The daily abuse started from around 4:30 to 5:00 a.m. when the *Stubediensts* (room servants) blew earsplitting whistles, cursed and screamed at us to get out of our bare bunk beds. Given that no one had a watch, we never knew the time, but like early cave men, we got ever better at guessing it.

Shortly after wake-up, we received a lukewarm, black, *ersatz* coffee made of roasted and burned roadside weeds, horse beets and who knows what else. We then rushed outside the barracks to line up five-in-a-row for the dreaded *Zehl Appell,* the counting of the inmates/slaves. The first count was by the *Stubediensts* and the second, by the *Blockaeltester*. These two counts took from 30-45 minutes.

The camp *Schreiber* (camp secretary, the official inventory slave-keeper), a tall, trim and handsome Polish gentile *haftling,* who was likely a Polish political prisoner or homosexual, then performed the third count of the morning with his rough and ready assistant. He was the official entrusted by the SS with keeping the number-records of all the *haftlinge* in the camp. The *Schreiber*, holding his clipboard with pages showing the long list of numbers of the prisoners in each barrack, always accompanied the SS-men.

However, this particular camp *Schreiber* was not fluent in the German language. As a result, I repeatedly received severe beatings from his brutal assistant during my first week in Jaworzno.

My crime was that I did not understand the Polish numbers the Schreiber quickly read off his secretarial pages, i.e., his slave inventory ledger. When he yelled out my *haftling* number, A-9561, in Polish, it sounded something like: *"Á gewengishond pinch sheshgishond yeden."* I did not know that this was Polish for the numbers tattooed on my arm. So when I did not immediately respond *"Jawohl!"* (Yes!), I received severe head, neck and body beatings from his assistant's nightstick.

As a non-Jew, the *Schreiber* was a privileged person. He was entitled to call out our "name numbers" in Polish instead of German, and his trusted assistant was entitled to provide us with truncheon thrashings as he saw fit. After a number of severe beatings, I and other non-Polish speakers painfully learned those Polish number sounds, even though we did not understand or even know the words for the individual numerals.

Finally, 30 to 60 minutes later, as we continued to stand at attention at the same spot, two or three SS men took the fourth morning count.

Anyone coming late for the roll call, regardless of the reason, was usually beaten so badly that even if he survived, he was not likely to live long after that. This was a grim and deadly game, and the Germans played it with full power, making up the rules as they went along. The SS were continually eating away at our well-worn nerves.

The repetitive morning body-counts were intended to quadruple-check whether anybody had run away during the night. If someone was missing, the whole camp paid a heavy and bloody price in various ways.

In addition to the body count during *Zehl Appell,* our tormentors were looking for anyone who appeared weak, sick, or had any questions or complaints. They immediately separated them and ordered them to step out of the lineup. Sometimes they would tell the complainants, "You will be sent to the infirmary." I did not know then, but found out later that this comment meant that the men were taken to the gas chambers and crematoria in Auschwitz-Birkenau.

There was no real infirmary for us in Jaworzno. A band-aid, a disinfectant, a temporary splint, a few stitches in our torn flesh, or a couple days of bed rest were the most a *haftling* could count on.

I clearly remember the dreadful terrible evening when, upon our return from work, the incoming slave count at the Iron Gate revealed that three or four *haftlinge* were missing.

As punishment, the SS cancelled our supper and forced us to stand at attention for several hours until they ascertained that the missing men were Ukrainian prisoners. The SS was determined to find out who had seen them disappear when we had crossed a certain suspected wooded area. Additionally, they wanted to know who might have helped them during their escape.

In order to extract information from us, the SS made us kneel on the raw ground for about one hour. After that, they ordered us to get down on our hands and knees, and form a solid human platform with our backs, necks, and heads. Three SS men then danced on our bodies, digging the heels of their boots into our backs, while beating us with their nightsticks and whips, splattering our blood and tears onto the ground. I ended up that night with five blue welts across my neck and back, and two boot-heel wounds on my buttocks. That evening, the Germans presented us once again with one of the many versions of Hell they had so malevolently created here on earth.

Several evenings later, as we arrived from our work at the electric power plant, the SS ordered us to a slow crawl and had us march through the far section of the camp, where the blood-soaked bodies of the runaway men were hanging from freshly placed wooden poles. The blue and black broken faces of the men were a clear indication that SS had sadistically tortured the men before shooting them. As can be expected, the sight saddened us gravely and frightened us to the core. The SS intended for every one of us to see the ultimate punishment for an attempt to escape.

Finally, for the fifth count of the morning, we would stop at the iron gate where two SS gate-guards counted us once again. We would then be marched out of the camp to the construction site.

On the march to the construction site, a group of armed SS men and their German Shepherd dogs guarded us from all sides, while cursing, shouting and beating us at will. We had to be at the work area shortly after 7:00 a.m. and we were then separated according to our work assignments.

A typical workday lasted for nine to ten hours. The main aim of the Germans was to squeeze all possible work benefit out of us and slowly deplete our life through forced hard labor and starvation.

At noon, we received a small bowl of soup with some potato pieces, horse beets, and sandy, grass-like material floating in it. Our sweat and tears dripped into the soup as we hungrily guzzled it up.

We stopped work in the evening at about 5 or 6 p.m. They counted us again before we set out on the 4-5 kilometer (2-3 mile), hour-long march back to the camp. Upon arrival, before we crossed through the iron gate of the camp, the SS gate-guards counted us once again, after which, they had us cross through the gate, and then dismissed us to our barracks.

A short time after our return from work, an appointed crew would go to the kitchen and bring back large canisters (galvanized milk-cans) of soup for each barracks.

Shortly afterwards, we received a third to a half of a small loaf of black bread. Each portion was supposed to weigh about 200 grams. Additionally, we received what the Germans called a *Zulage* (bonus), a small flat square of margarine or jelly, measuring about 1.25 by 1.25 by 0.5 inches.

If the smallest morsel of bread or jelly dropped to the filthy, muddy earth, we hurriedly picked it up, dirt and all, and put it in our mouths without hesitation, swallowing it eagerly, with zest. It was as if we had just saved a piece of a priceless family heirloom. This piece of bread was all we received for the next 24 hours, so we always had a mental struggle with ourselves whether to eat it all at once or to save some of it for the next morning or lunch — with the possibility of losing it during the night or during the long march to work the next morning. These daily decisions were dreadfully difficult and had life-endangering consequences.

By diabolical and purposeful German design, our striped pajama clothes had no pockets. If we wanted to save a piece of bread for the next day, we had to keep it inside our striped shirt, next to our bare skin, hoping that our pants rope would hold it from falling to the ground and getting lost. We had no cupboards or any other storage place. As with most decisions in those days, we rarely if ever knew whether we had made the right one. In addition to our terribly difficult physical and mental circumstances, the rules of our existence changed continually, from day to day and from minute to minute.

Except for special situations, such as when the Ukrainian men escaped, we usually could count on getting some food three times a day. The portion of food in Jaworzno was larger than in Auschwitz-Birkenau. For a couple hours of each day, we had something in our stomachs to soothe our nearly constant, gnawing hunger.

One late evening as we were returning from work, we saw a farmer's wagon drawn by a single horse. We soon noticed that the horse had slowed to a crawl, breathing with difficulty and gasping for air. Minutes later, the horse lay down on the road and placed his head flat on the pavement, clearly living its last moments.

About three days later, along with the usual grassy and sandy things floating in our soup, we found tiny pieces of meat. We all agreed that these meat scraps were from the horse we had seen on the road, falling to its knees, a few days earlier. We conjectured that the Jaworzno townsfolk were simply not hungry enough to eat that old horsemeat.

A specially-assigned *haftling* maintenance group kept the open-air latrines scrubbed clean and spotless, but there was no toilet paper or running water. The first couple of months in Jaworzno I was lucky. I managed to steal some scrap paper from the torn cement bags, and hide it between my striped uniform and my bare skin, for later latrine use.

Of the 3,200 to 3,500 Jaworzno inmates, some 85% of the concentration camp's population were Jewish civilians from a large number of European countries, and they represented a wide assortment of occupations. They included shoemakers, bankers, farmers, teachers, peddlers, doctors, plasterers, taxi drivers, insurance salesmen, watchmakers, rabbis, sheet metal fabricators, electricians, salesmen, bakers, bookkeepers, storekeepers, pharmacists, and more.

The rest of the camp inmates were a mixture of captured Allied POWs, homosexuals, dissidents, and various criminals. As mentioned, the POW (prisoner of war) inmates were jammed in with us, because the German Army Command had no compunctions about violating the Geneva Convention, which required them to provide special POW camps and treat captive soldiers as decent human beings. The Germans did not reckon on being defeated in World War II. They did not anticipate having to answer for violating their signed commitments regarding the Geneva Convention, and for all their other beastly deeds.

On a late summer evening, as I was walking to the far side of my barracks toward the latrine, I saw two *haftlinge* in their mid-thirties bargaining with each other over a single cigarette. As I stopped to observe, they concluded the deal. The buyer pledged half of his next day's supper in exchange for that single cigarette today. Both men appeared as frail, hungry, scrawny and emaciated as I was.

Privileged jobs, such as a *Kapo* (Work Group Leader), *Blockaeltester* (Block Elder), *Stubedienst* (Room Servant/Assistant), *Schreiber* (Bookkeeper) and *Uberseher* (Supervisor), were available according to rank, based on ethnic background. First in line were the so-called Aryan-Germans, followed by mixed Germans, then gentiles, and lastly, Jewish *haftlinge.*

These jobs granted significant benefits, such as physical safety from beatings and abuse, better supplies of food and water, and avoidance of dangerous or deadening physical work. More to the point, these privileges often meant the difference between life and death.

Since we all wore the same pajama-striped uniforms as all the *Kapos, Blockaeltesters, Stubedienents, Schreibers, Ubersehers*, it was hard to know who it was inside any given striped uniform. Therefore, any conversation with a fellow *haftling*, and even the tone in which it was held, could have important ramifications regarding one's survival immediately, the next day, or anytime later. One had a better chance of surviving if one was aware of the chain of command and all possible human connections and rankings within the camp system.

The prisoner population of Jaworzno represented people from diverse backgrounds and ethnicities. It is interesting to note that Aryan Germans discriminated against Gypsy Germans, even in Jaworzno. I recall several occasions when a German Kapo or a German SS said to a scrawny German assistant supervisor, *"Och, du kleiner Zigeuner Schweinehund...reih dich ein,"* meaning, "Oh, you small Gypsy pig-dog, get in line." These types of remarks would sometimes reveal who these Germans were in their former civilian lives. Additionally, it was psychologically remarkable that, even though both men were inmates of the Jaworzno Concentration Camp system, one felt the need or inner urge, to abuse the other.

It was generally rumored that inmates in the Jaworzno Concentration Camp system younger than age 13-15 or older than 50-55 would be automatically shipped to the gas chambers and crematoriums of Auschwitz-Birkenau. Indeed, very few men who looked younger or older than this age-range were visible, and if they were, they did their very best to hide it. Their very lives depended on it.

Jaworzno was a well-organized German chamber of hell, where, despite the three miserable meals a day, one became weaker from day to day. Prisoners, with numbered tattoos on their arm, were allowed to exist only if they were ready to work as slaves 9 to 10 hours a day, building concrete structures or roads, fashioning concrete beams, or digging black coal from the intensely coal-dusted and dangerous mines of Upper Silesia.

Any man with a noticeable wound or infirmity discovered by the SS, soon disappeared from the Jaworzno Concentration Camp. The SS quickly sent off these unfortunates to Auschwitz-Birkenau for annihilation.

During my incarceration, I saw several men shot point-blank, and I witnessed men brutally beaten until they died in their suffering.

Enduring Jaworzno

Jaworzno was a massive physical and mental torture chamber, where ultimately each haftling had one of three choices:

1) Make a run to the electrified fence and be free of worries and hunger pangs.

2) Slow down on your constant efforts to survive and take the beatings until death arrives.

3) Persist against all odds, safeguard your body, and aggressively struggle to survive.

I chose the third option.

In order to safeguard my body, I learned to be visually alert. I observed how others received bruises, wallops, and broken bones — and worked hard to avoid being the next victim. I was wholly consumed — every waking minute — with the effort to survive. My quest to survive compelled me to focus and actively search for ways to make myself invisible — or as low profile as possible.

I continually reminded myself of my father's last command, to return home and reunite with my family. With that in mind, I learned not to volunteer for anything, and made a conscious effort not to be on an outside line during the *Zehl Appell* or when marching to or from work. I made sure never to be first or last in the food line. These measures, I felt, gave me a better chance of avoiding the German shepherd dogs and the German SS human beasts with their Billy-clubs, whips and guns.

Had I believed the gloomy rumors in Jaworzno regarding the fate of my parents and siblings, I surely would not have survived.

One hot evening in July, as I was resting and sitting on the grass between the barracks, a young man from the next barracks came over and asked me to help mediate a problem. His assigned partner, with whom he had to share his bread, always argued with him about who had the larger part of the bread. The dispute seemed to worsen from day to day, he said, and he did not know what to do about it.

I showed him how to make a simple scale from a piece of thread that I pulled from my jacket-seam and a short piece of fallen twig, which I picked up from the grassy floor. He thanked me profusely.

Before he left, he quietly confided in me that he had been a Rabbi in a small town in Hungary. He asked me not to tell anyone, lest some camp official use it against him.

There was actually a swimming pool in the middle of the Jaworzno concentration camp, protruding halfway above ground. I never saw anyone swimming in it, though it is possible the SS used it for swimming and recreation during the hot summer nights. On the other hand, it may have served as a drinking water reservoir or possibly as a water source to extinguish fires.

Occasionally, when Hersh Baer and I got very thirsty, we took a chance and snuck up to the pool for some much-needed drinking water during the hot summer nights of 1944. This was a grave violation of the rules that governed our lives, as the SS forbade us to leave our barracks at night.

The bottom line was that with the limited possibilities available in that hellhole, one could only try to survive, one day at a time. Looking a day ahead was often beyond our vision or capability. Personal luck, fate (see *Talmud Bavli*, *Bava Kama* 60), visceral actions, and perseverance had a large role in one's survival.

I have no pictures to show, but I was but a skeleton and barely a human-appearing youngster by the end of the summer of 1944. In my stubborn and youthful mind, I tried my best to hold on to a glimmer of hope that I would be able to go home and reunite with my family.

During my *haftling* days in Jaworzno, all power of life lay in the hands of the German, Ukrainian and Polish SS. They enjoyed full freedom to kill and abuse us, any way they saw fit.

The Gray Silk Shawl
"Kamiah" disappears

As I described above, on the day the Hungarian government forced us out of our home in Vásárosnamény and drove us into the Ghetto of Beregszász, my Father had given me and each of my family members then present, a piece of the Gray Silk Shawl — which I knew as the *"Kamiah."*

Toward the evening of my arrival in Auschwitz-Birkenau, someone ordered our selected group of about 120 to 150 younger men to undress, toss our civilian clothes and shoes onto an existing large heap of clothing, and walk away stark naked into a nearby alley.

Of the numerous items that fill a young man's pockets, I made a quick decision to save only a small swatch of the *"Kamiah."* To save that small piece of silk in Auschwitz-Birkenau was no simple matter. I therefore schemed to remove my shoes and socks very slowly, and while in a bent over position, I pulled the swatch from my pocket, tore it and dropped most of it to the floor, managing to hide a small sliver of a piece in my hand. Furtively, I rolled up this tiny piece as tightly as I could and slipped it inside my mouth, hiding it in the pouch of my cheek for temporary safekeeping.

This was my "big secret." This small wad of the original 'silk shawl' became my emotional and physical connection to my family. It was my reminder of those extraordinary and fateful minutes in Vásárosnamény when my siblings and I stood frightened and motionless before our pain-stricken and distraught parents. My continued possession of this link with my family provided me with much-needed psychological comfort.

I managed to hide this tiny bundle of treasure alternately

behind my belt, inside my cheeks and under my tongue. After several months of this hiding scheme, I awoke one morning in Jaworzno to find that the "Kamiah" had disappeared.

I was stunned, scared, and relieved all at the same time. Stunned and scared, because I had become so attached to the "Kamiah" and wondered how I could manage without it. But I was also relieved because I would no longer have the daily complexities of watching over it 24/7.

Hiding from reality — Living on hope

Just as in Auschwitz-Birkenau, I, along with a good number of inmates in Jaworzno, did not want to admit to myself or acknowledge to others that the Germans had gassed and burned my parents and family upon arrival in Auschwitz-Birkenau. We stubbornly held on to our mistaken belief and concluded with some satisfaction that such a mass-murder could not have been possible.

We simply refused to process such a monstrous concept. We did not want to. With so much daily anguish and hardship already on our plate, we had no room for more. We were neither prepared nor able to deal with such immense trauma and pain.

This attitude made it possible for us to struggle through the daily abuses we suffered at the hands of the Germans and their assorted henchmen.

As inmates in Jaworzno, we had no proof of the "Holocaust" since we never really saw the greater picture. In spite of the many horrific rumors, we hid from reality, and concluded to our minds' satisfaction that such an enormous slaughter of our people was not possible.

I constantly yearned for my family and the pre-war days in Vásárosnamény, dreaming of the day when our entire family would be together again. This dream kept me going, and became almost an obsession. It was my fervent hope and wish that my parents and siblings were alive somewhere, somehow. I could not afford to lose the power of this underlying hope.

Psychiatrists may well identify and explain these instinctive, youthful notions and this self-protecting approach during my confinement in the monstrous Jaworzno Concentration Camp, as 'willful denial.' Indeed, there seems to be no limit to the human mind's capability to deceive or justify itself.

As a naïve and innocent teenager, I must have needed that denial in order to go on and continue with my struggle — one more day at a time.

Perilous Silesian coalmines

By mid-October 1944, I could no longer deal with the severe cold weather conditions in the open-air construction site. The flimsy pajama-type clothes could not protect me. The cold winds and intermittent rain had taken their toll on my body. In addition, malnutrition had caused a severe drop in my blood circulation. The skin color of my hands, forearms and legs, all the way to the tips of my toes, had deteriorated to a dull, pale white.

I was no longer able to warm my limbs. I had become a bundle of skin-and-bones, someone the SS had a special term for, a *"Muselmann."* There appeared to be no escape from death, but I was determined to fight it with all the energy remaining in my bones and the consciousness in my mind.

During an evening conversation with my friend Hersh Baer, I told him of my decision to try for a transfer to work in one of the coal mines. There were two nearby, the *Carlsgrube* (Carl's Mine) and *Friedrichsgrube*. I heard from other inmates that while the work in the 1,180-foot-deep mines was hard and dangerous, the temperature was steady at about 52 degrees Fahrenheit — much warmer than the open-air construction site where I worked. After receiving some advice from another inmate as to how I might get transferred, I walked over to one of the barracks and registered there with the *Blockaeltester* for work in the mines.

When I got down into the mine my first impression was one of bewilderment at its unexpected large belly, so deep in the ground. It seemed as if half of the coalmine could easily blow up without the people in the other half ever hearing about it.

The staging area was quite massive and screechingly noisy. It was huge and was peppered with numerous pajama-clothed inmates like myself. A group of civilian dressed engineers, elevator operators, the SS guards, as well as lots of deafeningly noisy equipment, were at all key positions.

At loading times, there were about 18 young *haftlinge* vigorously working in the entry, and at the cart switching-loading and elevator shaft areas. I heard from my new co-workers that those fast-moving cart-switching machines had torn many a *haftlinge* worker to shreds.

The mine had three overlapping work-shifts to produce the maximum amount of coal. Each shift worked 9-10 hours each day. This was a bad mine. The air was thick with coal dust, making breathing difficult. For six days a week, layers of black coal-dust and soot covered our faces, bodies and clothes. The *haftlinge* were provided no safety equipment, no hard-hat protection against falling coal, no miners' flashlights and no dust-proof facemasks. Only the SS, engineers and company officials were supplied with protective equipment.

The mine was some five kilometers (three miles) from the concentration camp. The walk to work took us over an hour, but we usually returned to the camp by means of some kind of local mini-freight-train, which stopped and unloaded us near Jaworzno. To keep myself safe in the mine, I kept to myself and

pretended not to notice anything, keeping myself as incon-
spicuous as possible.

"Luxury" store in Jaworzno

Upon returning from the coal mine one evening, our group received special recognition. The cluster leader jubilantly announced a historic "first." His face lit up in joy as he stated
that, in appreciation of the large volume of coal we produced,
the company we worked for (I don't know if he mentioned its
name) was giving us German Reichsmarks, which we could
spend in the camp store, known as the Kiosk.

Before this announcement, I had not been aware that
there was a kiosk in Jaworzno. However, upon inquiry, I
learned that this tiny kiosk, the only one in the camp, was
open each Sunday for a few hours. I was also told that it was
for the exclusive use of the Aryan *haftlinge* with legal access to
German Reichsmarks, as well as the SS, Gestapo, and the various company and management personnel. The Aryan *haftlinge*
were able to receive German currency or checks in the mail
from friends and family. Someone further explained that, a
small select group of German and Polish-Aryan inmates had
special privileges, allowing them to receive censored mail and
money from a pre-approved list of family members and
friends.

Early the next Sunday I went with great anticipation with
my hard-earned German Reichsmarks to purchase something
to eat. Having no pocket or purse, I had securely hidden the
cash inside my jacket, at my navel. I do not remember the face
value of my German currency.

Much to my chagrin, I found that for the most part, just a
small stash of Polish cigarettes, cigars, chewing tobacco products, and shaving paraphernalia were displayed in the kiosk.
They also had a few German and Polish greeting cards, statio-
nery, envelopes, German postal stamps and a number of

junky-looking "luxury" gift items. I had absolutely no use for any of those. My eyes searched for some food that might fill my empty stomach to stop the gnawing hunger pain in my gut.

After anxiously gawking at the German and Polish printed descriptions on the packages, the closest thing I could find that looked like food was a can of mustard, something I had never seen or eaten before. My German Reichmarks were just enough to buy the largest can on display. I immediately hid the can inside my shirt, so as not to conflict with any possible camp rules, or lose it to someone in authority — meaning, anyone with a title, or anyone stronger than me.

Upon my successful return to the barrack, I proudly showed off my exotic food purchase to Hersh Baer. Sitting on the edge of his bunk bed, the two of us contentedly transferred the whole can of strong mustard into our empty and shrunken stomachs.

As can be imagined, the painful after-effects of that mustard "meal" were so strong, that for more than 20 years after my liberation from the concentration camps I was unable to consume even a small amount of mustard.

A Special Day: An SS bayonet pierces my chest

Most of us were not aware of calendar dates during our captivity in Jaworzno. Each day was just as dreadful as the previous one. There was no reason to make any special effort to remember one day over another. Moreover, we had no pencil, no paper, no calendars, no watches and certainly no appointments. Therefore, most of us did not know the calendar dates. As we looked at each other's skeletal and decrepit bodies wasting away within our striped *haftling* clothes, there was not much assurance that we could survive another month, another week or even another day.

Yet, one day in Jaworzno emerged as a particularly noteworthy one, as inmates whispered to each other, "Today is December 31, 1944." The day started out as something unique because many of us hoped that following the end of this worst-ever year in our lives, we would be treated the next day to the start of a better one.

Rather unexpectedly, scores of *haftlinge* began to share their reminiscences of their families, their former homes and lives. Somehow, the atmosphere and individual feelings seemed different, and some of us even tried to smile at each other.

We openly yearned for our families, for our freedom and even for physical luxuries. We whispered about them to work comrades and even to casual acquaintances we recently met in the camp. A friendlier, more hopeful and reserved but upbeat atmosphere developed for the day.

However, for me, it turned out to be a special day of quite a different kind. On this day, I felt the sharp tip of an SS bayonet piercing my ribs. In fact, I had a very direct, near-fatal confrontation.

My troubles began in the early evening, after I finished my day shift in the coalmine. Typically, as we marched "home" to the Jaworzno Camp, our group stopped at the camp gate for the usual SS body-count. As we crossed the gate into the camp, our tired group was abruptly stopped. Two supervisors began to randomly heave men out of our standing line. I, too, was grabbed by the collar and forcibly pulled out.

After about ten minutes, someone explained to our segregated cluster of men that the coalmine was short of workers, and soon after our supper, the SS would take us back to work the night shift. However, he quickly added, with self-assurance, "We will be given a second supper for working a double-shift."

I must admit that the 'second supper' felt good. It was the very first and only time since I arrived in the Auschwitz-Birkenau and Jaworzno hellholes that my stomach was actually full. Our small, separated work group felt that we had happened upon a stroke of good luck, and we smiled at each other with the satisfaction of a full belly. At any rate, we had absolutely no say in the matter, because when the SS said, "You are working a second shift today," they weren't asking for our opinion.

For obvious reasons, the coalmine security personnel did not train or trust any of us *haftlinge* with the use of explosives. Instead, their trusted German civilian "explosives-master" made the rounds and blasted the coal for our area of the mine. The coalmines were deep in the belly of the earth with solid coal walls all around us, which needed continuous blasting.

After the explosives expert blasted enough coal for me to shovel into the coal trolleys, he left my workstation and went on to blast the coal for the next *haftling.* As usual, I was alone for the difficult job of hand-shoveling the coal into the underground narrow-track coal trolleys.

However, on Dec. 31, 1944, by the time I returned to work for my second shift of the day, I could not overcome my lack of sleep and extreme exhaustion. Though I was not hungry for the moment, my arms had no strength for a second shift of coal shoveling.

Therefore, while the heavy coal dust settled from the explosives-*misters'* blast, I decided to sit down and take a couple of minutes' break. But before sitting down, I decided to leave a historical note, a cryptic message of my presence in this coalmine. I simply wrote the date and my initials: "December 31, 1944, A.Z." Writing these words gave me an uplifting feeling of boldness and possession. The crayon I used for this memento was a chunk of the plentiful black coal on the mine floor, writing onto the gray granite wall of the horizontal coalmine shaft in which I was working. As there was no one in sight, I sat my exhausted body in the corner of the coal-vein on a low granite ridge. I have no recollection of lying down on the ridge.

Suddenly, I awoke to a sharp pain and a weighty pressure in the center of my chest. As I opened my eyes and tried to raise my head and take a look at my rib, I saw a shiny bayonet press-ing at my aching chest. Instantly, my eyes followed up the bay-onet and discovered an angry, sneering SS man with his finger on the trigger of his shotgun, looking me square in the eye and screaming, *"Wás ist lós!? Wás ist lós!?"* (What's going on!? What's going on!!?)

I froze in place. I did not dare move or even try to raise my head again. My instinct told me that if I would make the slight-est move, he would either push down on his bayonet and pin my chest to the granite ledge or just pull the trigger and shoot me on the spot.

After a breath of silence, I started pleading. I explained to him in my finest German that the camp was short of men, and that this was my second shift for the day. I begged him to for-give me. After repeating my most earnest pleas four or five times, exhausted and scared to death, I fell silent.

As he continued to stare down on me, I tried to read his mind through his cynical and snide "I got you" look. I desper-ately tried to interpret from his wide smirk whether I had got-ten through to him, but I had no clue.

After what seemed like infinite silence, he abruptly jerked the bayonet from my rib and proceeded in a heavily Ukrai-nian-accented German to severely curse my mother, my fa-ther, and me. He ended with, "Don't you ever do that again, you shitty Jew!"

He then stood-by for a few minutes as he ordered me to work double-speed, and watched me load the coal trolley at a pace I had never previously matched. Finally, he left my station to continue his checkup tour of the other slaves in the dusty coalmine.

Surprise: Salvation in the infirmary

According to rumors, there were around 3,200 to 3,500 male *haftlinge* in Jaworzno during my time, but there was only one infirmary, and it was intended for minor body repair problems only, such as small cuts, bruises, a bloody nose, a few stitches, a temporary splint, and at best, a couple days of rest.

In the back area were a number of rooms that served as temporary confinement cells for the severely injured, such as men with a broken arm or foot, the severely weak, the badly beaten, or anyone with internal ailments or a contagious disease.

The infirmary was not there to save them. These patients were regularly collected for their one-way ride to the gas chambers and crematorium. The SS trucked these unfortunate *haftlinge,* estimated at about 75 to 120 each month, to the Auschwitz-Birkenau gas chambers to be gassed, choked, and then burned in the nearby crematoria. Consequently, few people were willing to risk using the infirmary for anything other than minor problems.

By late autumn there was a new rumor circulating in the camp that the SS was no longer sending our people to the crematoria. Rumors, good or bad, were our only source of information. Though this rumor turned out to be true, we had no way of knowing that at the time.

I continued to work day or night shifts in the coalmines until about January 11, 1945. However, due to my severe malnutrition and utter weakness I decided to take a risk, and went to the camp infirmary hoping to get a few days' rest. I had no energy left in me to shovel coal even one more day.

The doctors were busy. I stood in a waiting line for about 20 nerve-wracking minutes. When my turn came, I slowly approached the standing doctor, pointed toward my stomach, and said in German, "It hurts." He ordered me to drop my pants, looked at my totally bare body for one second, (we had no underwear), shook his head and told me in German, "You have a hernia and you need some rest." He pointed to an empty bunkbed in the far corner and sternly ordered, "Get in there!" As it turned out, he therewith saved me.

There were three Jewish doctors in the infirmary. I recall that one was from France, the second, a Dr. Pavel (or Powel), was from Czechoslovakia, but I don't remember the third one. The doctors looked just like us. They wore the same striped prisoner clothes as we did, but they received sufficient and better food and had much better working and sleeping conditions than we had. Nevertheless, they too lost all their families upon arrival in Auschwitz-Birkenau, on the same selection line as all the rest of us.

We later learned that during late autumn of 1944, the SS leadership in Auschwitz-Birkenau realized they were about to lose the war. They tried to cover up some of what they knew were their worst crimes against humanity. To that end, they ordered a select group of *haftlinge* to hurriedly dismantle and destroy evidence, particularly the murderous gas-shower chambers and the crematoria. This cover-up attempt was the real reason that the Germans stopped trucking our sick people from Jaworzno to the gas chambers of Auschwitz-Birkenau.

Moreover, to eradicate any evidence of the dismantling of these crematoria and gas "shower rooms," the SS murdered nearly every one of the prisoners they forced into the dismantling project.

I soon realized how fortunate I had been that the doctor assigned me to an infirmary bunkbed during his superficial, two-second hernia diagnosis. I do not believe I would have survived the imminent forced evacuation of the concentration camp, which became known as the terrible "Death March" that began in January 1945.

Liberation: The brave and victorious Russian soldiers

A few days after my admission to the infirmary, we began to hear muffled sounds of distant bombardment, mingled with faint booms of thunderous army cannons. Oh, what magnificent welcome sounds they were to our ears! They were truly the most joyous and melodious sounds we had heard since arriving at this monstrous place called Jaworzno. During the anxious days in the infirmary, this lovely cannon-music provided us with substantial signals of the approaching Russian Army and our hoped-for liberation; they were sufficient to enable us to daydream about our imminent freedom.

On or about January 17, 1945, apparently following orders from the Central Camp Command in Auschwitz-Birkenau, the Jaworzno SS leaders ordered the camp to evacuate. Their intent was to try to escape the advancing Russian Army.

We became aware of the evacuation plan when three armed SS men came into our corner of the infirmary and ordered us to get dressed. They said they would be back in an hour and that we had better be ready to go on a march with them.

When the SS men left, those of us in the infirmary were puzzled and bewildered. We did not know what to make of this stern, unexpected command. Luckily, there were among us a captured Russian army officer and a former Polish army soldier. Their unambiguous and definite advice was that we should not go with the SS, no matter what they told us. They felt intuitively that the SS would just kill us on the road. The older and more mature inmates amongst us agreed with them, that our chances of survival would be greater if we stayed put in the infirmary.

On the other hand, some younger inmates felt that we must go with the SS. They firmly reasoned that we had no power to refuse, and that the SS would simply beat us until we would follow their orders. They also suspected that the Germans would blow up the entire camp before they left, thus killing us in the infirmary. Lastly, the younger ones felt that the SS were likely to shoot us all before they left, in order not to leave live witnesses to tell the Russians about the bestial German behavior.

After a seemingly long whispered planning session, we all decided to stay and take our chances. When the SS men came back to march us out, they found us lying in our bunk beds, saying we were sick and unable to leave the infirmary. Fortunately, they gave us no threats, not even arguments. They let us stay in the infirmary and left without a word. I do not know what happened to the inmates of other areas in the infirmary, but for us, our decision saved our lives.

It was already late night, when we looked out of our dark infirmary window into the well-lit camp command area and saw the last columns of our brothers marching out of the camp. We watched from a distance as the SS padlocked the two large steel gates of the camp from the outside, entered their jeeps and three-wheeled motorcycles, and disappeared into the darkness of the night.

But that was not the last we saw of the SS. Two days later, three SS men returned, riding their three-wheeled motorcycles into the camp, and loaded up provisions from the locked basement storage-area of the infirmary. They then came into our infirmary room and repeated their order that we must go with them. Once again, we told them we were sick, had fever and were unable to walk. Fortunately, after some relatively mild threats, they left us in the infirmary without harming us.

The noises of thundering rockets and cannons became

louder and stronger, a sure indication that the Russian Army was coming closer to our camp. By now, the township air raid sirens were blaring several times a day, and we began to hear airplanes over our camp and bomb blasts in the general area. From our window, we really could not make out whether the thunder and rumbling came from German or Russian sources.

Locked inside the camp, we felt all alone and worried. As far as we could see through our windows, there were no SS soldiers around, but we dared not go outside to check, lest we find ourselves being shot at. Still another concern was that the SS might have booby-trapped the infirmary doors and the camp area, so that we would blow ourselves up if we tried to leave.

The SS had left us in the infirmary without any food, and we were getting very hungry. We searched the kitchen area and shared whatever scraps we found. As our hunger intensified, we decided to brave it and searched the infirmary basement storage-rooms for food. We managed to break locks and cabinet doors and found some food — small amounts of flour, cereal, honey and margarine that had been left behind. This provided some relief for our stomachs, and helped us emotionally as we silently waited for the war to pass over our heads.

Every time we heard those booming sounds in the distance, we clapped our hands and smiled broadly at each other, as our weak hearts pounded away in anticipation. Our minds were on an emotional high, while our bodies needed urgent medical help, not to mention that our growling and shrunken bellies were clamoring for some decent food.

The following two days, the sharp crackling and whistling sounds of gunfire outside our camp replaced the deep thunder of the cannons. The seasoned Russian and Polish soldiers among us quickly identified these sounds as coming from close combat between the advancing Russian army and the retreating German soldiers.

By this time, we felt sure that our days of captivity were approaching their end and that our freedom was close at hand.

On January 27, 1945, the brave Russian soldiers broke open the camp gates and set us free. I estimate that there were about 25 to 30 survivors in the Jaworzno Camp infirmary. The Russian-speaking inmates explained to them our sad situation. The Soviet soldiers were friendly and concerned and gave us some of their dark brown bread and warm army food. They pulled up a traveling two-wheeler army canteen into the Jaworzno Camp, and we helped ourselves. The canteen food looked very much like a homemade Jewish *cholent* (stew), consisting of a weighty mixture of colorful beans, potatoes, onions, garlic and chunks of real beef.

The Russian soldiers were still in the midst of a protracted war so they could not take time to care for us, nor could they provide us with clothes or medical assistance. With tears streaming from our eyes, we expressed our deep appreciation for liberating us and for their generosity with their food.

It was not until the summer of 1945 that I learned from Jaworzno Camp survivors, that the camp evacuation had become a terrible "Death March." During the course of the march, the SS shot and killed most of the Jaworzno inmates.

The survivors described their terrible suffering on the "Death March." The SS marched them in the sub-zero weather of January, February and March of 1945, while the winter snow, rain and wind ripped their shoes off their feet, and tattered their meager clothing. During most of the march, they received food only once a day. The German and Ukrainian SS guards shot on the spot any inmate who stopped to relieve himself or to care for frostbite sores or anyone who slowed down due to lack of energy or even to help another *haftling*.

During their night stops, the SS forced the "Death March-
ers" to sleep in hay lofts, barns and even open fields. They
marched them to the concentration camps of Béchamel, Gross
Rosen, Buchenwald, Flossenburg and deeper into Germany.

The "Death March" clearly reflected the deep-rooted and
fanatical hate of the German and non-German SS men. They
were eager to kill Jews even at this late hour, knowing full well
that they were doomed to defeat and were approaching their
own downfall at the hands of the victorious Allied forces.

The SS must have felt and clearly seen the imminent col-
lapse of their devil's kingdom, and yet, they madly went on
with the mass murder of their Jewish and non-Jewish captives
with heightened speed and redoubled effort. The German
fiends remorselessly murdered anyone they determined to be
unworthy of life in their eyes.

On Jan 27, 1945, the Russian Army liberated the
Auschwitz-Birkenau concentration camp complex.

Caught wearing Wehrmacht Army uniforms

Several days after the victorious Russian Army set us free in
late January 1945, some of the daring infirmary inmates
wrapped themselves in flimsy blankets and walked out of the
camp to search the nearby village for food, shoes and warm
clothing.

Upon their return, they excitedly talked about their great
find, a bombed-out German freight train just a couple of miles
away, which contained brand-new *Wehrmacht* (German Army)
clothes. Next to food, warm clothing was most important to
us.

Other than our thin pajama-like camp uniforms, all we had
to wear were the hand-stitched flimsy pants and jackets that
we had hurriedly cut and hand-sewn during the past few days
in the infirmary. We had cut these so-called clothes from SS

blankets and had roughly stitched them with spools of thread we found in the infirmary. They looked like potato-sacks, rather than jackets and pants.

When we heard of this opportunity to obtain decent, warm clothes, half a dozen of us joined the rush to find the railroad train full of garments. As we scouted around, searching our way to this treasure, several Russian infantry platoons passed us on the road. The soldiers paid no attention to our skeletal group, wearing potato-sack outfits. As for us, we felt reasonably safe roaming the deserted streets, content with the knowledge that the Russian soldiers were here and in control, and that the bestial Germans were gone, driven out of sight and out of our lives.

After searching about 25 minutes on the streets, the sight of the bombed-out train full of brand-new *Wehrmacht* army clothes greeted us. Some of us quickly discarded our hand-stitched potato-sack clothes and put on the brand-new, oversized and ill-fitting German *Wehrmacht* uniforms. Others pulled the uniforms on top of their potato-sack costumes. Then, for good measure, we grabbed as many uniforms as our weak arms could carry, to take back and share with our *haftlinge* brothers who were too weak to walk out to the train. As it was getting close to dusk, we were in a hurry to get back to our infirmary barracks with our load of new garments.

We were within close proximity to the Jaworzno Camp when a company of marching Russian soldiers stopped us and began questioning us suspiciously, thinking they had come upon a group of German soldiers trying to escape. With a mixture of Polish, Russian, and German words, we tried to explain our sad situation, while repeatedly and furiously pointing to the concentration camp tattoos on our arms. But, the Russians were not convinced. They leveled their bayoneted guns at us and ordered us to march ahead of them to their superior officer in a nearby private house.

Trembling with fear, we repeated our story to the Russian

officer. The officer, who spoke some German, checked the tattoos on our arms, looked at our emaciated faces and bodies, and asked us for details about our experiences.

He must have believed us because he did not have us shot. However, he ordered us to drop all the extra clothes we were carrying and to immediately take off the German army uniforms we were wearing. He then ordered our small group, some of us now half-naked, to hurry back to the Jaworzno Camp.

By this time, it was pitch dark on the streets. We were all terribly frightened by this experience and frozen stiff from exposure to the bitter cold. We felt utterly stupid and yet very lucky. After this frightening escapade, we were delighted to be back with our liberated friends in the camp, even though we were without the new *Wehrmacht* Army clothes.

❦ 4 ❦
After the War

Return to Vásárosnamény — by foot

In the waning days of January 1945, World War II was still raging on all fronts. The German/Hungarian military partners and their various allies were slowly retreating, but still putting up a strong resistance. All through the unforgiving cold winter of 1944-45, the Russian Army did its best to drive the Germans and Hungarians and their criminal partners back towards Germany, Austria, France, Hungary, Holland, etc.

In the meantime, by the end of January, I found myself among the fortunate small group of Jaworzno infirmary inmates to be alive and free. It was a sensation that is hard to describe. My new-found freedom felt strange. It was as if I was drugged, removed from reality. I felt like I had woken up from a bad dream. My mind refused to acknowledge that I was stuck in a foreign country, in decrepit health, with no funds, and with WW II raging all around me.

I clearly remembered my father's last instructions to our family upon our arrival at Auschwitz-Birkenau when we fearfully disembarked from the cattle boxcar trains. He had emotionally whispered to us, "As soon as we get through this, write to Szécsi Károly in Tiszakerecseny, and make sure you come home. We will meet at home. Don't go anywhere else. Just go to Vásárosnamény and let us wait for each other at home."

Oh, how I dreamt of that moment and waited for it throughout the terrible hardships. Now that I was free... every fiber in my body wanted to follow those deeply stirring and inviting instructions. Only one thing really mattered to me now — to rush home and meet my separated parents and siblings!

Not wanting to waste any precious time, I was determined to start the long, uncharted trip home immediately. However, in my youthful teenage enthusiasm, at the age of 17½, I failed to take into consideration a host of important issues:

1) The extremely long distance from Jaworzno, Poland, to Vásárosnamény, Hungary.
2) The brutal winter crossing of the Carpathian Mountains into Czechoslovakia, en route to Hungary.
3) My total lack of cash, food, winter clothes and shoes.
4) That World War II was still raging throughout Europe.
5) That the Germans had destroyed all my identity papers in Auschwitz, leaving me with no way of proving who I was, where I had been, or what citizenship I held. It was common knowledge, that a basic requirement for life during wartime was the ability to prove one's identity. Lacking that, one would likely wind up in jail or possibly be shot on the spot.

None of the above seemed to trouble my youthful and energetic mind. In my steadfast teenage determination, I refused to consider or reflect on any of these serious limitations.

Therefore, about five days after liberation, my first thought was to go to Krakow, the capital city of Poland, located about 50 kilometers from Jaworzno. My theory was that there would be refugee trains or freight trains running from Krakow to one of the large Czech railway hubs of Kosice, Chop or Bratislava. I was not fussy. Any one of these stations would do for me. I reasoned that if I reached Kosice, it would get me comfortably close to Vásárosnamény, about 90 miles (145 kilometers) away.

And so, on Feb 2, 1945, I was ready to move forward. Alone but determined, I started my trip in the direction of Krakow on foot. After half a day's walk in the snow, a sympathetic Russian oil-tank driver noticed my shaking outstretched arm: the typical signal for a request for a ride.

He stopped for a moment and without exchanging a word, he motioned me to climb atop his truck. I climbed up the freezing steel steps and lay face down on top of his ice cold oil tank as flat as I could. With both bare hands holding tight to the front railing, I was able to keep from being blown off.

Safe House in Krakow:
Jews in a danger zone again!!

Upon arrival in Krakow, I used the limited and heavily-accented Polish language skills I had acquired while listening to the babble of the Jewish-Polish *haftlinge* that worked with me in Jaworzno. I randomly approached people on the street and asked for directions to a Jewish school, a synagogue or some Jews. Before long, a sympathetic man guided me to the second floor of an apartment house at *Dluga Ulica, dwanáscie* (Dluga Street 12).

It turned out that this was a "Jewish safe house" run by former Polish-Jewish fighting-partisans and a few recently returned concentration camp survivors from the area. They magnanimously provided free shelter and basic food staples to the small trickle of returning Jews from the various concentration camps and war-partisan groups that fought and sabotaged the German Army in southern Poland. I stayed there overnight.

The safe house administrator hastily informed me, in Yiddish, of the need to keep the doors locked securely and to gather Jews quickly off the streets of Krakow. I did not want to believe him when he listed the many physical dangers to Jews in newly-liberated Poland. He emphasized that Polish anti-Semites did not like the idea of Jews returning alive from concentration camps and were especially irate that some returning Jewish citizens had the nerve to re-enter and reclaim their former homes and businesses.

Writer Jan T. Gross describes the above in his book, *"Fear: Anti-Semitism in Poland after Auschwitz."** Upon return to their former Polish homeland after World War II, 1,500 Polish-Jewish war partisans and concentration camp survivors were murdered. Unpredictably, the surviving Jews' fatal error was to try to return to their former homes, farms, and businesses to claim what was lawfully theirs. Many Polish anti-Semites did not like that idea, to the point that they were willing to murder the legal owners.

During my next day in Krakow, I attempted to gather train information. I walked to the station and talked to the railway manager and conductors about travel to Czechoslovakia. To my dismay, the repeated answer was that the tracks from Krakow to Tarnow were still bombed out, but that the trains were up and running from Tarnow to Kosice, Czechoslovakia.

I had no map and was not sure whether the railway officials were steering me correctly. One of the safe house elders came to my rescue. He had an old, well-worn map of Central Europe, and he helped me note the main railroad stations I would need to traverse in order to reach my destination. He confirmed on his map that I would have to travel from Krakow to Tarnow, then on to Nowy Sácz, and then to Stáry Sácz. From there I would need to cross the Polish border into Czechoslovakia and go on to Kosice and Chop. Finally, I would have to cross the Czech border and catch a train to Vásárosnamény, Hungary.

I had nothing in my pockets, no earthly possessions of any type, not even paper or pencil. I therefore etched the names of those cities permanently in my mind.

By nightfall, I found a Jew from Budapest wandering around in the Safe House. He was about 30 years old, reasonably older than I, which gave me a sense of security. I do not

---

* Random House, June 2006

remember his name. He had walked to Krakow from the recently liberated Plashov Concentration Camp, only nine kilometers away.

During our conversation in Hungarian, it did not take long to discover that he, too, was in a great hurry to go home. Like me, he was eager and restless to find his extended and missing family.

I informed him of my earlier visit to the railroad station, where I had learned that the railways in Tarnow were in operating condition. As there was no way for us to confirm this information, we chose to believe it was true.

We decided to walk together to Tarnow — some 90 kilometers (56 miles) away, in southern Poland — where we hoped to catch a direct train to Kosice, Czechoslovakia. From there we would go our separate ways to our respective homes in Hungary.

We started our march on the main highway with a small amount of food, generously supplied to us by the concerned Safe House manager. Once on the road, we went from house to house, knocking on doors, begging for food and a place to warm our frozen bodies. And so we walked along or, more correctly, since we both were frail and could not really lift our feet much, merely trudged along the snowy roads to Tarnow.

Most residents and farmers refused to unlock their doors for us. Some resentfully gave us some food, cold water or a warm tea. Others invited us to warm up at their fire. The biggest problem was that every night we needed both food and shelter, a combination which was exceedingly difficult to find. Nevertheless, we were determined to go forward, begging along the highway. We managed to find our daily food and shelter and continued toward Tarnow.

On the war front, the German and the Hungarian Nazi armies were retreating, while fighting hard and slowing down the Russian army. The fighting front must have been raging not very far from us, because every so often, we heard loud sounds of cannon fire. We encountered many Soviet Army trucks and speeding troop carriers moving from place to place along the main highway, but they did not bother us. We were simply two shaggy-looking, rag-covered, skinny men plodding along in the deep snow. We appreciated the wide tire tracks the Russian Army trucks created for us on the snowy and frozen highway, which made our trudging easier.

On the third day of our slow walk, a strange medical predicament arose. As we walked slowly in the blizzard, my partner suddenly yelled, "Where are you? I can't see you!" He stretched out his arms and started to stumble. I soon discovered that he had developed snow blindness. Neither of us had ever encountered this type of problem. From then on, he walked close behind me and tried to make use of my footsteps in the snow, as he hung on to the back of my shabby blanket-coat.

Language, too, became a problem because my walking partner spoke only an elite Hungarian dialect, about ten words of German, and not one word of Polish or Russian. Therefore, I had to do all the begging for food and getting instructions and road directions, by using my Hungarian-accented German and otherwise improvising when necessary. However, because we were in Poland, where most natives hated the Germans, I used the German language as a last resort only.

In retrospect, I fully recognize that we acted irrationally and with profound negligence to undertake such a trip without a proper plan. We were in precarious health, and placed our very lives in danger. It would not have taken much effort to kill us or maim us for life. Our beloved familys would have totally lacked any clues as to where to begin searching for us.

Delicious cheese noodles
served in carved table holes

Neither of us had a watch to tell time, but when it started to get dark, we knew it was time to hunt for a night's rest and food. One night, the nearest farmhouse visible on the horizon was very far from the highway. We hesitated to go that distance in the deep snow just to have another door slammed in our faces, but there was no other house in sight, so we took a chance.

That night we got lucky. I distinctly remember the Polish farmer welcoming us into his house as though we were his long-lost cousins. In spite of our unfortunate appearance, which must have been shoddier than that of normal beggars, he had us join his family at their supper table. Sadly, due to our Polish language limitations, friendly conversation was not feasible.

At first, we sat apprehensively at the table because we feared that this super-warm welcome might be a cover-up for some trap waiting to ensnare us. The warm human hospitality just seemed too good to be true. It was like a merciful and astonishing dream.

After a short and anxious wait, the farmer's wife brought a large pitcher of warm milk from the next room, and everyone poured himself a tall glassful. The farmer picked up his glass and wished us good health in Polish. Out of normal courtesy and due to our lingering safety concerns, we waited impatiently until the man, his wife and three children drank the first third of their glasses.

His wife soon left the table and returned with a serving plate of thick slices of farm bread and a plate of butter. Finally, she brought in a large pot of steaming hot, delicious-looking noodles and cheese and placed it at the head of the table in front of her smiling husband. At this point, our fears of food-poisoning tricks or foul play had completely disappeared.

She did not bring in any plates. Instead, we ate the noodles and cheese out of carved shallow hollows in the thick, wooden dining table. The farmer's family and the two of us filled ourselves, and there were still noodles left in the pot. After supper, his wife took dripping wet linen towels and wiped clean the table's carved-out holes.

After such a delicious and filling meal, the man of the house handed us two thick, colorful farm blankets. We put one on the mud-covered hard kitchen floor and covered ourselves with the other. Both of us slept extremely well, alongside their coal-heated oven.

In the morning, they generously gave us a breakfast of milk with bread and butter. After our profuse thanks and blessings, they provided us with directions to the snow-covered highway. We anxiously followed their instructions and continued our long and determined walk toward Tarnow.

We were delighted and relieved when we finally arrived at the Tarnow railroad station. However, a sad surprise awaited us. Contrary to what I had been told, the solitary station attendant informed us that the railroad tracks were still bombed out. He optimistically advised us that we should walk to the next large city, Nowy Sácz, where he knew "for sure" that the trains from Poland to Czechoslovakia were up and running.

But upon arrival in Nowy Sácz, we heard the same depressing story again. We were severely saddened by these repeated letdowns, but since we were not about to turn back to Krakow, we decided to continue the seemingly endless, frozen walk to Stáry Sácz.

Russian Jewish Captain in Stáry Sácz

As we trudged through the city of Stári Sácz, we nervously and repeatedly asked for directions to the railroad station. Suddenly, two armed Russian Military Policemen approached us and asked for identity papers. Perhaps they thought we were runaway German soldiers dressed in rags just to hide our real identity.

Of course, we had no identification papers of any kind. In broken and minimal Russian and Polish, I tried to explain our tragic situation, but they did not seem to like my story. They then turned and questioned my road partner. Since he was only able to speak to them in Hungarian and a few words in German, they marched us to a nearby massive private house. We passed a number of gun-toting guards, and finally, on the third floor, we faced the commanding officer for interrogation.

I nervously repeated three or four times to the Russian captain that we were Jews from the German concentration camps and that we were trying to go home in search of our families. We also persistently showed him the tattooed numbers on our arms.

Suddenly, he seemed to become enraged and screamed in Yiddish, *"Az du bizt a Yid, red tzu mir Yiddish!"* (If you are a Jew, talk to me in Yiddish!) Upon regaining my lost breath and confidence, I proceeded to have a ten-minute conversation with him in Yiddish. I told him about my extended family and our miserable captivity in the Nazi concentration and murder camps.

After that bit of dialogue, he gave each of us a warm hug, called to his assistant in the next room, and ordered him to write our names, a few words about our predicament, and that we are searching for our families, on two blank sheets of paper. The captain then signed the certificates, stamped them with a large triangular Russian Army stamp and handed us the freshly penned documents.

He then explained in Yiddish that the triangular stamp would get us through any Russian checkpoint. "You see," he said, "most of my men don't know how to read, but they are first-rate and reliable soldiers, and they know the value of the triangular stamp." He then reached into his desk, pulled out a liter bottle of whiskey, and handed it to us. He advised us to walk out of the city to the main highway and by waving the bottle, flag down a Russian military truck going all the way to

Kosice, Czechoslovakia. He repeatedly cautioned us not to go with any truck, unless it went all the way through the Carpathian Mountains to Kosice.

The next day, we followed the captain's instructions. We walked out of the city to the main highway and selectively waved the whiskey bottle whenever a likely Russian truck approached. Eventually, we did entice a Russian military truck driver, who gave us a ride through the snow-packed Carpathian Mountains to the outskirts of Kosice. As he turned off the main highway to his army supply area, he gave us directions to the city's railroad station, and we wished each other a warm *"Dasvidaniya"* (Goodbye/until we meet again).

The two of us walked for another couple of hours until we reached the Kosice railroad station where we separated. By this time, my road partner's snow-blinded eyesight had returned to normal. He soon continued his rush to Budapest to find his family, while I sped off to my former home in Vásárosnamény.

I happily rode on top of a freight train from Kosice to Chop. There were no trains going from Chop towards Vásárosnamény, so I walked and hitchhiked on horse-drawn carts and farm wagons pulled by slow-moving teams of oxen.

On February 28, 1945, after twenty-four difficult winter days on the road, I finally arrived at my former hometown, Vásárosnamény.

Father's cousin, Dezső Zelcer

Upon my arrival in Vásárosnamény, I stopped passersby on the main street and inquired about Jewish families in town. To my delight and surprise, someone directed me to Dezső (David) Zelcer, my father's first cousin.

Unfortunately, Dezső's parents passed away when he was a teenager. In the 1920s, when Dezső was a young man fresh out of school, he lived with my family in Vásárosnamény for a short time. For a few years, he worked as a part-time book-keeper in my father's leather business, and later he kept the books for the Zelczer bakery.

During the 1930s, Dezsõ opened and operated a fully-stocked, modern haberdashery. He carried an up-to-date, top-quality line of merchandise, which he displayed in the latest and most modern glass-displays of those days. His elegant store was located in the best part of town, in the Vásárosnamény commercial center. His warm customer service with his ability for friendly conversation attracted a wide assortment of the intelligentsia, and many well-to-do customers frequented his store.

Dezsõ was among the few Jewish men to return alive from the insufferable *Hungarian Munkatábor Service* (forced Army Labor Camp), which the Hungarian Nazi Government had formed several years earlier for Jewish men of military age.

Around September of 1944, the advancing Russian Army had liberated Dezsõ and his severely abused Munkatábor group. He had been home for five or six months by the time I arrived.

The last time I had seen Dezsõ was about two years prior, in 1943, when he was home in Vásárosnamény to visit his family on a two-day furlough from his army service in the Munkatábor. It was great to see him again — and this time around, he was a free man.

Nevertheless, it was a somber letdown for me that neither my parents nor any of my siblings were home to greet me. My exhausting rush to come home through the Carpathian Mountains in the bitter cold of February, 1945, had ended without the hoped-for results.

I found Dezsõ extremely depressed, lonely and noticeably hurting. He was palpably angry and anxious. His bitter conversation and cynical demeanor clearly demonstrated his deep distress and unmitigated fury at Hungary and the entire world.

Dezsõ had married the beautiful Elza Frankel, from

Olaszliska, (b. 1909) in the mid-1930s, and they were the parents of a lovely daughter, Anika (Leah). After incarcerating them into the Bregszasz ghetto, like all Jewish families of Vásárosnamény, the Germans murdered Dezso's wife and young daughter upon their arrival in Auschwitz-Birkenau.

Dezsõ received me warmly and tenderly. He gave me nourishing food and a warm bed. I stayed in that bed for six consecutive days and nights. I just ate, slept, rested my tired feet, relaxed my exhausted body and slowed down my speeding and tortured mind.

After living through the nightmares of the Beregszász Ghetto, the treachery in Auschwitz-Birkenau, the cement/concrete construction and the coal mine of the Jaworzno Concentration Camp, and finally the 24 bitter cold winter days on the Polish and the Carpathian Mountain roads, my legs and arms had shriveled and looked like four skinny sticks. It seemed that even without an X-ray, one could clearly see the details of my elbows, knees and joints under my paper-thin skin. During the following weeks, Dezsõ fed and nursed me back to health and put some decent clothes on my back.

Many weeks later, we heard rumors that in Mátészalka, a city about 14 miles (22 kilometers) away, kosher meat was available. Actually, there was none for sale. Instead, we had to bring our own chicken, duck, or goose to Mátészalka. One day a week, a *Shochet* was available for kosher ritual slaughter. Dezsõ made the food arrangements. We koshered his kitchen, and a semblance of a kosher Jewish home began to appear.

After I regained my health, Dezsõ kept me occupied with various jobs in his sundry business endeavors. Table salt was so hard to find, that it had become a precious commodity in our area of *Bereg Megye* (Bereg County). Skilled at business, Dezsõ wanted to offer this item to his customers. In late April of 1945, he sent me with a hired driver to the city of Satu Máre

(Satmar), Romania, to pick up a wagonload of table salt that he had ordered. The experienced wagon driver had two fast horses, so we made the 35-mile trip (56 kilometers) in about six hours, each way.

Dezsõ entrusted the money to me, and I placed the bundle of cash in a small pouch suspended around my neck and hidden inside my shirt for safekeeping. Since neither party needed a record of the transaction, Dezsõ instructed me to give the cash to the seller only after the correct number of salt bags were fully loaded and properly camouflaged on the farm-wagon.

At this point of World War II, the Russian and Allied armies were still engaged in heavy fighting and had much German territory to conquer. The war was raging in various parts of Germany, Hungary and France, and the Russian army was not interested in enforcing national borders between the countries it had freshly conquered from the German and Hungarian armies.

As a result, most of the newly liberated borders between Hungary, Romania, Poland and Czechoslovakia were wide open. Therefore, many smart businessmen, like Dezsõ, were able to easily move merchandise across these borders, satisfying people's dire needs during this period of shortages of food and supplies.

I recall another occasion when Dezsõ sent me with a bundle of cash to pick up a wagonload of soap. He purchased the soap from a dealer in Nyirbátor, about 28 miles (45 kilometers) away, and I brought the load of homemade, light-yellow soap securely to Vásárosnamény.

During the course of 1945 and 1946, a small number of Bereg Megye survivors trickled back into town from the various concentration camps and from the Displaced Person camps in Germany, Austria and France. They, too, were searching for their family members, neighbors, and lost friends. Unfortunately, most of them came in vain. Very few survived the Nazi murder machine.

Like Dezsõ, the very small number of Vásárosnamény-area Munkatábor returnees tried to settle back into their former towns and houses. A few of them reopened the businesses they or their parents had run, anxiously awaiting the return of their loved ones. They did not want to take a chance on missing them.

Several returnees, along with a number of fair and friendly Hungarian gentiles, did their best to cooperate with the Russian military authorities in their efforts to apprehend and convict some of the mass murderers and former leaders of the Hungarian "Arrowhead" Nazis of the Bereg Megye area. Somehow, most of the Arrowhead leadership seemed to have disappeared after the war and succeeded in avoiding prosecution.

As for me, it was only several months after the German surrender of May 8, 1945, that I began to realize the extent of the devastation and destruction the Jewish People had suffered. Then, my teenage mind finally accepted that most of my family was not returning from this catastrophe. I felt crushed and depressed all over again.

Károly Szécsi revisited:
Invitation to a family feast

About five weeks after my unceremonious return from the Jaworzno Concentration Camp, our genuine family friend, Mr. Károly Szécsi, sent me a message via Dezsõ. Mr. Szécsi lived about 16 miles (25 km) away in a small town called Tiszakerecseny. His message was actually an invitation to his house to meet his family, at which time he would host a special family meal in my honor.

At this point in the still-raging European war, in early April 1945, the Germans and Hungarians and their Axis partners were losing badly but were still fighting the advancing Allied armies on many fronts. Food was in very short supply all over Europe.

The Szécsi family, living in a small farming town, had no such problems. They had a modest farm and raised their own chickens, geese, and ducks. Additionally, Mr. Szécsi was always ready to trade his General Store's merchandise with farmers who often preferred to pay in farm goods and did not wish to deal in the fast-devaluing Hungarian pengõs. Therefore, the Szécsi family did not feel the food shortages that had been widespread throughout Hungary since 1938-1939.

My arrival at the Szécsi home was a significant occasion, and the family received me with open arms. Their welcome was not so much for me personally but rather for the son of an old friend, my father, whom they sorely missed.

Mr. Szécsi did not press me with questions as to where I had been, what terrible things I had seen, or what had happened to my parents and siblings. Nor did he refer to his pre-Ghetto visit to Vásárosnamény when he made his noble offer to hide our family at grave risk to himself and his family.

Mr. Szécsi saw that I was sad and hurting, both mentally and physically. In a most caring and fatherly way, he said to me, "Sándor [my Hungarian name], tell me what you want to tell me." I truly appreciated his utmost sensitivity as I was both unwilling and unable to talk about my parents or siblings, the many cruel things I had seen and the pain I had experienced.

In the name of my parents and family, I profusely thanked him for his caring and benevolent offer to save us in the spring of 1944. I did not, and really could not, get into a discussion about my parents' refusal to accept his lifesaving offer to save our family.

Mr. Szécsi served a fine table wine before, during, and at the end of the large family meal. As usual, he was a thorough 'gentleman' and a true friend of the Zelczer family.

The next morning, after a sumptuous early breakfast, Mr.

Szécsi packed for me the valuables my parents gave him for safekeeping in the spring of 1944. My parents entrusted them to Mr. Szécsi, when he made his surprise visit and heroic offer to save us, just days before our brutal Hungarian government forced us into the Ghetto of Beregszász.

Mrs. Szécsi, Károly's gracious wife, packed up a basketful of delicious food for Dezsõ and me. After my sincere thanks, I somberly returned with my family belongings to my elder cousin in Vásárosnamény.

Sign of life from my sister in Bergen-Belsen

During the early summer months of 1945, my brothers, Herman, Mike, and sister, Helen, straggled home from their tormenting concentration camp experiences. They arrived physically abused, sickly and emaciated but, nevertheless, in various stages of recovery.

One early morning in August of 1945, a messenger knocked on our door in Vásárosnamény. The courier loudly announced that he had been sent by Mr. Károly Szécsi to deliver an important postcard that had been addressed to him in Tiszakerecseny.

The postcard was from our sister Ruci (Szeréna). She mailed it to Mr. Szécsi in fulfillment of our father's last instructions in Auschwitz-Birkenau to make sure to contact our good friend Mr. Károly Szécsi in Tiszakerecseny.

The postcard contained but a few essential lines. Ruci simply stated that the British army had liberated her, and she was recovering in the Bergen-Belsen Displaced Persons (DP) Camp,* in the British-occupied zone of Germany. (Bergen-

---

* Bergen-Belsen was the largest such camp in Germany, with a special section for Jews — 11,000 of whom were housed there in 1946. The camp was vacated by 1951, with the majority of Jews having made Aliyah to Israel.

Belsen was the largest such camp in Germany).

Suddenly, our hearts over-flowed with anticipation. One more member of our family was alive! The good news expanded our horizon and instilled renewed hope. Since I was the youngest and most daring in the family, I volunteered to take on a cross-borders journey to Bergen-Belsen to bring our sister home. During the course of the next week, I gathered travel information on how I might get to the Bergen-Belsen area. I also needed time to find out which of the numerous foreign borders might be open and which I would need to cross on foot, illegally by night.

In my small hand-sewn backpack, I took along a number of cartons of American cigarettes. Cigarettes, especially American-cigarettes, were the most versatile form of money. They spoke a language anyone could understand. Throughout war-torn Europe, American cigarettes were "king." People readily accepted them for payment of goods and services — often preferring them to the usually unreliable and deflated local currencies. It was truly amazing how in the midst of so much hunger, death and destruction, the addiction to cigarettes was so unbelievably high.

My planned trip was to take me from Hungary through Czechoslovakia, then through the Russian zone of Germany, to the American zone of Germany, and finally to Bergen-Belsen, located in the British zone of Germany, near the North Sea. This is why I sorely needed "multilingual" currency.

After days and nights of train hopping, I arrived in the Bergen-Belsen camp a day before Yom Kippur of 1945. The person in charge of the girls' recovery area told me that Ruci was recovering nicely, but she was still so weak that the shock of suddenly seeing me might be too much for her. She suggested that I wait a day or two, so she could break the news to her slowly.

The day after Yom Kippur, the supervisor called Ruci into her office, inquired about her family and asked if she had any brothers. After a pleasant "warm-up conversation," she called for me from the next room, and we were happily and lovingly reunited.

Later that day, Ruci despondently informed me of something she did not disclose in her postcard to the family. Our beloved and vivacious sister, Bina Rivka, had died a few days after their liberation. She tearfully explained that Bina Rivka's starved and emaciated body was too weak to fight off the typhoid fever, from which nearly every one of the Bergen-Belsen Concentration Camp inmates, including Ruci, suffered.

During my three week stay in the Bergen-Belsen DP Camp, I found four other recovering survivors, all girls, from Vásárosnamény and its vicinity. By this time, they all felt well enough to make the journey home and were excited to join us. They were anxious to get home and start the search for their own missing families. About one week after Sukkot, our small group of six set out on the railroad trip home.

Railroad service was poor. The trains were still running, albeit without enough conductors or proper timetables and with inadequate passenger cars. At times, they seemed to change directions at will. They repeatedly made long stops due to bombed railways and damaged bridges. Occasionally, they even ran out of fuel before reaching their destination.

Travelers waited day and night on the railroad platforms, hoping to be among the first in line for the next train going in their direction. Admittance to these platforms was hard to obtain. Large masses of people waited in the overflowing waiting rooms, in the hall areas and outside. People traded food for clothing and clothing for food, and both of them for cigarettes. Bribery for the purpose of getting inside the hall, to the platform or onto a waiting line, was rampant. Even ticket sellers openly took favors at their windows and issued tickets accordingly.

It was here that my American cigarettes worked their magic. In order to get close to the train platform area, I held a single pack of American cigarettes in my half-closed hand. This promise got all six of us admitted to the passenger waiting area. Once we were on the platform, we still had to wait endless hours. When the train arrived, the intense pushing, elbowing and shoving became quite dangerous at times.

We usually could not get onto the train the normal way. We often pulled or pushed each other through the train windows because the steps and entry aisles were solidly packed with people.

For the girls' benefit and security, we agreed on strict safety rules. We had to make sure that all of us were on board in a close cluster, in the same train car. We were quite aware that we could not afford to get separated from each other.

If not all of us could get on the same train car by the time it started to move, those who had boarded, jumped out through the window to rejoin those who were left waiting on the platform. Then we stood ready for the next train-boarding effort, often many hours or even a day later. We had to repeat this tricky process each time we changed trains.

We also had to be on guard at refueling stops because any railroad car or group of cars could easily be sidetracked and suddenly travel in a different direction. Some trains had to change direction due to bombed-out bridges or unsafe rail tracks.

Still another hazard was the wild, untamed and often brutal behavior of Russian soldiers on leave, particularly towards women. Vagrants, beggars and thieves were all around the platform along with numerous wounded war victims.

In short, it was clear that, for our personal safety, all six of us had to be within sight of each other.

Generally, the overworked conductors did not bother us. They slowly squeezed around us to collect fares or punch passengers' prepaid train tickets. We got by without paying by showing the tattooed numbers on our arms and explaining that we were on our way home from the concentration camps and had no money.

Occasionally, it took a few cigarettes to get a couple of so-called "reserved seats" to be freed up for the exhausted and still-recovering girls.

The American cigarettes also bought us much needed food along the way, as we had been unable to stock up in Bergen-Belsen for the long road ahead. After some five days of continuous day-and-night travel, we finally arrived safely in Vásárosnamény with a couple of packs of cigarettes remaining in my backpack.

Complex decisions in Vásárosnamény

In the spring of 1944, in those heartbreaking days when "our" Hungarian Government and its gendarmes forced us into the Ghetto, we were a family of eleven — two parents and nine children. In the course of the ensuing year of the German/Hungarian Holocaust, we lost both parents and four siblings. Fifty five percent of us were massacred. Only three boys and two girls survived. It was an outrageous and terrifying year.

Nevertheless, the Zelczer family's Ghetto and concentration camp survival rate of 45% was at least 4.5 times greater than that of the average Hungarian Jewish family. This astonishingly high rate of our survival was due to our ages — 16½ to 29 in the year 1944 — as well as happenstance (see *Talmud Bavli*, *Masechet Bava Kama*, p. 60a).

Physically frail and emotionally and mentally depressed, the surviving members of our family had trickled back to Vásárosnamény. Unfortunately, we found that during the year of our absence, our former neighbors had confiscated most of the Jewish homes in the Vásárosnamény area. Very few homes remained vacant from the time of our forced Ghettoization.

The second half of 1945 was a busy time for our surviving

family because it required our determined efforts to get our life re-started again. Only now do I realize the extraordinary courage it took for us to move forward from amidst the devastation. It was a complex process and required optimism and hope, as we had suffered such massive losses to our extended family. A giant leap of faith was required to pick up the broken pieces and reassemble the remnants of the Zelczer family.

After putting our heads together and airing our dilemmas, we decided to stay in Vásárosnamény. All five siblings agreed to make a concerted effort to refurbish our parents' home and restart their bakery business. Everyone pitched in and gave their undivided attention to putting things in order. We decontaminated the house, replaced the smashed and missing bread-making equipment, and attended to many other details. We slowly reopened the Zelczer Bakery and got the business off to a good start.

We reestablished our line of credit at one of the two local flourmills, which was our most important supplier. As a baker's proverb goes, one cannot bake bread without flour. However, due to the post-World War II food and money shortages, we did have to limit our supply of freshly baked goods.

Just like the Zelczer family, some Jewish DPs (Displaced Persons) returned to their former homes. However, they rarely stayed for long for a number of compelling reasons. I will attempt to list some:

   *   Typically, the Gentile family that illegally occupied a Jewish home refused to vacate the house. In order to gain entry to their former home or business, the returning DP had to file a lawsuit and bring the thieving occupier to court. Often, an anti-Semitic Hungarian judge made the official "court decision" featuring a long list of excuses, such as that the occupying thief had an entire

family in the house, while the Jewish 'claimants', who were the true owners, were only one or two surviving DP returnees. Therefore the judge often favored the occupying thief!

* During the owners' absence, the neighbors emptied the house of furniture, clothing, and belongings. The Jewish owners not only returned penniless but found their homes vandalized.

* It was difficult to return to a country that had so willingly deported one's family, who were lawful citizens, and knowingly handed them over to be murdered.

* It was emotionally wrenching and difficult to live among people (former neighbors) who had proven to be so hostile and treacherous to Jews. Also, there were no tangible indications that they would not repeat their murderous deeds.

* Many survivors were psychologically unable to live in their own family home; from which their loved ones had been so cruelly driven out and brutally massacred.

* In Poland, Jews became aware that Polish Gentiles killed over 1,500 Jewish concentration camp returnees *after the war*. Reclaiming homes and businesses became a life-threatening event.

* The neighbors and local citizens had frequently stolen the Jews' business merchandise, and the returnees had no money with which to stock up and start their businesses over again.

* While the Russian Communist Military Government did arrest, jail, and even execute a number of Hungarian, German, Polish, and Ukrainian Nazi leaders, they made only a token effort to pursue justice against Nazis who initiated, assisted and carried out the fatal expulsion of Hungarian Jewry to Poland, Ukraine, Austria and Germany.

* The Russian-occupied countries, such as Poland, Lithuania, Ukraine, Czechoslovakia, Bohemia, Hungary, Romania, and Yugoslavia, were placed under complete
Communist rule and lifestyle throughout 1945 and
1946. The Russians started to enforce their athe-
ist/Communist government and way of life, and were
much too busy to get involved in helping returning Holocaust survivors recover their farms, homes, jobs,
businesses and personal property. Also, for the long
run, a Communist regime would be too restrictive to
permit us to follow a ritualistic Jewish life.

Indebted to the Russians and Americans

Germany's well organized surprise military attack on Russia in
1941 caused the loss of vast Russian-controlled land areas,
the complete devastation many of its cities, along with the
death and wounding of enormous numbers of Russian soldiers and civilians.

However, this lengthy bleeding process also drained Nazi
Germany and its partner Hungary of their elite military forces
and caused serious shortages in their military supplies. Additionally, as the American and British forces arrived at Nor-
mandy on June 6, 1944, Germany was forced to divide its tired
ground forces into two major fronts — the existing Russian
front and the new American-British front. Therefore, Germany
was unable to fight 'successfully' on two such major fronts.

While I am no military expert, I am quite certain that without the brave Russian soldiers, the American and British Armies could very well have had a tough time against the Axis
powers.

Therefore, I personally owe the Russian, American, and
British armies my most sincere gratitude, deepest admiration
and greatest esteem. All of the concentration camp survivors

are deeply indebted to them for freeing and saving them from Nazi slavery and horrible death.

Had WWII dragged on just a bit longer, very few — if any — concentration camp inmates could have survived ... anywhere.

Last Three Straws:
Russian Communists

The very foundation of Communist/Socialist ideology requires the elimination of any and all religions, and therewith, the post-World War II Soviet-dictated Communist regime and lifestyle which took root in Hungary began to interfere with my daily Jewish religious life to such an extent, that I was not willing to accept it. My family was steeped in a strong religious faith and had a tradition of religious freedom. Atheism and Communism as a "way of life" were antithetical to my very existence.

For example, under the prevailing Soviet style Communism it became problematic to obtain a steady supply of kosher food, to have regular and open religious services and to keep the Sabbath as a holy day.

In addition, about a year after World War II, the Communists began to view us — this small vestige of Holocaust-surviving Hungarian Jews — as part of the enemy population, sabotaging their determined effort to 'Communize' Hungary.

In summary, this was another reason why most survivors did not wish to remain in Hungary, as well as in other East-European states.

In the ensuing months, three developments became the final straws in our decision to leave Hungary:

STRAW #1

One sunny day in early March 1946, as I was looking over our picket fence onto the pedestrian traffic on Vasut Utca (Train

Street), I noticed a group of five heavily-armed Russian soldiers marching down the street with their bayoneted guns held on their hips. From the distance, they appeared to be gathering civilian men off the street and marching them away as if taking them captive.

I crouched instinctively and got myself securely out of sight and rushed up to the attic to verify this nerve-racking scene.

Peeking down from the attic, I clearly saw the armed soldiers marching down the street and firmly ordering additional adult males to fall in line with their original captives. As I watched the bizarre scene through the small slanted roof window, I could not help recalling one of my mother's pre-World War II Saturday night stories, about teenagers and young men being rounded up in the street by the Russian Czar's army and not being seen again for 10 to 20 years, if ever.

STRAW # 2

Some months after we reopened our shattered bakery in Vásárosnamény, we began to feel ill at ease with our neighbors. Our good neighbors and former friends from before World War II had become estranged. We sensed that some of them were not comfortable with the fact that a tiny percentage of the former Vásárosnamény Jewish population had come back from the death camps to reclaim houses and reopen their businesses.

STRAW # 3

Finally, the sheer weight of the fact that a preponderance of the Jewish people had been brutally decimated in Nazi-ruled Europe had penetrated our conscious and subconscious psyches. We began to think rationally, examining our standing in the general community, and concluded that the relationship between the local population and ourselves had been poisoned so deeply, it had become irreparable.

The Departure

Adding it all up, we felt angry, resentful, and ready to leave behind our neighbors and former friends with their thieving fingers and bloody hands. We had reached a point of such high frustration and bitterness that we secretly prepared backpacks and prepared to leave.

One night in the late spring of 1946, after making inquiries about how best to reach the Austrian border, we — Herman, Mike, Szeréna, Yity Kleinbart (who had joined our family and planned to marry Mike), and I — packed a few belongings, put on our backpacks, turned off the lights at 2 a.m. and disappeared into the night.*

We boarded a train to Budapest, where we were greeted by our exuberant, friendly and charitable cousin Gaby (Gavriel) Salzer. He went out of his way to help us with proper legal documents, which enabled us to cross over the border to Austria. Gaby had an exceptionally warm heart and was helpful to everyone in need. He was my hero.

After some days in Vienna, we headed to the DP camp in Pocking, Germany, located about 40 kilometers from Munich.

Munkatábor Slaves

At about the time when Hungary joined the Axis Powers, its Nazi-oriented Government decided not to trust the Jewish soldiers and officers in its service units any longer. Consequently, they created the *"Munkatábor"* (labor camp) for Jewish soldiers. Then, the Hungarian government relieved the regular troops of all hard, dangerous and labor-intensive tasks and forced them upon the *Munkatábor* servicemen.

The typical *"Munkatábor"* work consisted of loading and unloading freight trains and trucks with ammunition and

---

* My sister Helen and her husband Mike Friedman, who were married in Vásáros-namény, decided to stay awhile in Hungary.

other supplies; constructing, repairing, cleaning and maintaining all types of roads and bridges; clearing mine fields, digging and filling trenches, etc.

The *Munkatábor* servicemen were forced to do all the above at a fraction of their former Army salary. Furthermore, they did not receive military issue clothes. Throughout their years of ordeal, they had to acquire their shoes, boots and all clothing at their own expense. Even their meals were cut to about half of that of the Gentile Army.

The Munkatábor men served in non-combat roles near all battle-fronts, under the command of the sadistic anti-Semitic Hungarian army officers, in a wide range of locations throughout Russia, Poland, Ukraine, Hungary, Germany and Austria.

Although at the start of their military service, these men were healthy and fit soldiers, nevertheless there were very few *Munkatábor* survivors. It is estimated that only 7 percent survived the war because of the horrific and deliberate abuse meted out by the Hungarian army officers. It would seem that they were striving to prove to their German partners that they were their equal in brutality, abuse, hate and murder.

From the second half of 1944 through the first third of 1945, the Russian Army liberated small groups of the severely abused *Munkatábor* servicemen. They were the lucky ones, because the Russians allowed them to go home to search for their families.

But those who remained under the command of the Hungarian army were in big trouble, because during this time period the Hungarians handed over some of them directly to the concentration camps, and some to the German army, which also delivered them into the Nazi concentration camps. The Hungarian army thus dumped the abused *Munkatábor* servicemen from the proverbial "frying pan into the fire."

Brother's escape

My usually tight-lipped older brother, Herman, told me about his amazing escape one winter night in 1944, near the town of Doroshitz, Ukraine.

There were a reported 950 Jewish servicemen in his *Munkatábor* battalion, all jammed into a corral and a complex of farm buildings and haylofts. On this particular freezing winter night, due to their additional work assignment, Herman, with his 8-man work detail, arrived late from their assigned station.

Upon arrival, they found all gates to the corral locked, and the armed Hungarian guards would not let anyone in or out. In addition, because they were late, they did not receive their usual meager supper.

Unable to get in, they dejectedly walked away and lay down outside in a nearby field under a bare tree. Luckily, they carried their thin covers in their backpacks, so Herman and one of his friends spread one cover on the snow and the other on top of them. They kept each other warm enough to keep from freezing to death by huddling together.

However, they woke up abruptly during the night and saw 25-foot- high flames engulfing the corral and its buildings. From a distance, they saw the circle of Hungarian officers and guards standing by, their guns drawn to prevent any escape. Officers and guards watched gleefully as they burned to death all the *Munkatábor* servicemen they held captive.

Another detail, Herman recalled, was a description of the Hungarian *Munkatábor* "work platoon." Among their typical daily jobs was loading and unloading freight trains, digging foxholes for the Hungarian and German soldiers, clearing minefields, building and repairing roads, abutments, bridges and railroad tracks. All jobs were carried out in their personal private clothes, amidst terrible hunger and other hardships.

The Hungarian army made sure to accomplish its mine-field-clearing jobs in a most bestial manner. "They forced about 20 of us to hold each other tightly," my brother said, "arm-in-arm and shoulder-to-shoulder, making us march for hours and hours across all suspected mine fields and roads, while the brave (!) Hungarian army officers and soldiers walked behind us at a safe distance with their guns aimed at our backs. I lost a good number of my *Munkatábor* friends that way."

Four categories of concentration camps

The Nazis operated an assortment of concentration camps, and it is important to understand the operational differences among them. The camps can be divided into four categories, as follows:

1. EXTERMINATION/GENOCIDE AND WORK-TO-DEATH CAMPS
These camps were a means of destroying as many people as possible, and Jews in particular, in the shortest possible time, and at the least possible cost to the German Reich's murderers. In Auschwitz-Birkenau, they mass-murdered by gassing their victims in large fake-showers and then speedily burned them in crematoria. Typically, they accomplished most mass-murders on the very day of arrival, unless the eight gassing-shower rooms and the 46 ovens were in use, in which case the intended victims would have to wait a few days or weeks.

In other murder camps, the Germans, Ukrainians, Hungarians and Poles mass-murdered men, women and children by gassing them inside hermetically sealed shipping vans and trucks, and by shooting men, women and children point-blank over open graves and pits. In some locations, they were left outside to freeze to death, or were drowned. At others, they buried their victims alive.

At various concentration camps, in addition to mass annihilation, work-to-death measures were adopted, such as in some sections of Auschwitz-Birkenau in southern Poland, in Bergen Belsen near the North Sea in Northwestern Germany, and in Dachau, located in southern Germany. Additionally, there were a number of combination murder and work-to-death camps located in or near towns and river areas of the Ukraine, Poland and Russia.

2. WORK-TO-DEATH SLAVE LABOR CAMPS

After my initial incarceration in Auschwitz-Birkenau in Poland, I was transferred to a slave labor camp of the second type. This work-to-death camp was located outside the town of Jaworzno, in Polish Silesia which the Germans termed, Oberschlesien. I have previously described the miserable daily subsistence there.

Truckloads of inmates, who had been worked nearly to death, were regularly shipped from the Jaworzno concentration camp back to Auschwitz-Birkenau for mass gassing and burning. On their return trip, the SS trucks replaced these victims, the "used-up slaves," with fresh new arrivals of captured *haftlinge*, who would then be similarly enslaved and maltreated unto death. In the German language, this process was simply referred to as *Vernichtung Durch Arbeit*, "Extermination Through Work."

These camps were intended to squeeze the most work possible out of the slaves for the benefit and profit of the German civilian and military authorities, working us to death amidst terror and starvation, drowning us in pools of our sweat and blood. These concentration camps and murder sites were located all over Germany, Ukraine, Austria, Poland, Russia, Holland, Italy and Czechoslovakia.

3. "SHOW" CONCENTRATION CAMPS

These concentration camps were few and existed for a number of populations, such as select groups of Russian, Dutch, American and British POWs, as well as certain children and Gypsy

(Roma) groups. There were also special concentration camps for specific nationalities which the Germans created for possible "hostage trading" for high-value German captives.

However, shortly after the "show and tell" performance for the Red Cross inspectors, during which the camp had accomplished its political and/or financial aim, the Germans then usually murdered the unfortunate *haftlinge* imprisoned in these camps. The Red Cross, falling for these Nazi deceptions, readily delivered truckloads of free food and medical supplies to these camps. Of course, all of these supplies went straight into the hands of the S.S and the German Army.

4. KASTNER'S "TO PALESTINE" GROUP

Lastly, there was a special concentration camp set up in the periphery of the Bergen-Belsen Camp for 1,684 assorted Jews, including about 40 leading rabbis and their extended families. These were all members of *"Kastner's to Palestine Group"* that paid a high blackmail price to get out of Hungary, under the pretext that they wanted a "safe passage to Palestine." The majority of these *haftlinge* had sufficient cash and jewelry to pay the extortion fee to travel to Palestine and survive.

The SS held them for a number of months in a special Bergen Belsen non-working-camp until the full ransom of dollars, gold, and jewelry was delivered to Adolf Eichmann and his SS lieutenants.

Inmates in this concentration camp benefited from five life-saving privileges:

1) They received three meals a day, seven days a week.
2) They were not required to do any physical work.
3) Their entire families, young and old, stayed together throughout their ordeal.
4) They were allowed to keep all personal effects.
5) They wore their personal civilian clothing throughout their confinement.

Once Eichmann and his SS cohorts received the full payment, they issued a release order, and the Escape Train received permission to enter Switzerland and to continue from there to Palestine.

Dire need for DP (Displaced Person) camps

Yes, World War II was over. The Germans, and their European Axis partners were soundly defeated and surrendered unconditionally to the victorious American, Russian, and British Armies. Appropriately, the world named this day of May 8, 1945, "VE Day", standing for "Victory in Europe Day."

However, the cessation of fighting brought with it the urgent need to house, feed, clothe and medicate the massive number of civilians made destitute by the war and in desperate need of basic human necessities. The human casualties were very high everywhere ... but they were over 90% among the Jewish population. While there were many in dire need, I will concentrate on the Holocaust survivors.

Many concentration camp *haftlinge* had been liberated inside the camps in which they had been enslaved. Also, the SS abandoned scores of captives in the midst of their murderous "Death Marches." Others were abandoned in open freight and cattle trains, in train stations, in isolated farmers' barns, or on highways and empty fields. And finally some *haftlinge* were simply abandoned by the SS at the very last minute when the SS decided to change into civilian clothes and hurry into hiding.

All the survivors urgently needed food, clothing, shoes, housing, and immediate medical attention.

Following the end of WWII, DP camps were created in previous German Army bases, Army training camps, and sometimes in or near former Concentration and Extermination

Camps. A few DP camps were established in France, Holland and Italy, but most were located in the American and British zones of Western Germany and Austria.

In these camps, the survivors were able to organize themselves, find food and limited health care, and more. In order to facilitate rehabilitation, vocational training and repatriation, various cultural and religious populations were housed accordingly, forming temporary DP communities.

The victorious American and British authorities were assisted by many able charitable groups such as UNRRA (United Nations Relief and Rehabilitation Administration), the Joint, (American Joint Distribution Committee) and HIAS (Hebrew International Aid Society). Additionally, many smaller organizations provided vital and gracious help.

While a majority of the liberated men and women did not want to return to their former homes and countries, a number of them did go back, primarily to search for their lost families. The small number of Munkatábor survivors opted mostly to join the concentration camp survivors in the DP camps.

The survivors of the Zelczer family were among those who at first returned home but later changed their minds and left. We gravitated to the DP camps in the American-occupied Zone of Austria and Western Germany. I believe there were from 200,000 to 300,000 Jewish DPs scattered in these camps. We were the surviving remnants of the once flourishing Jewish communities of Poland, Germany, Austria, Hungary, Romania, Ukraine, Czechoslovakia, Lithuania, Holland, Belgium, France, Yugoslavia and other European countries.

Most of my surviving family found shelter in the Pocking DP camp, located outside the town called Pocking, in southern Germany, about 40 kilometers from Munich. My recollection is that in 1947, there were around 7,500 displaced persons in this camp. We languished aimlessly in these DP camps, with no clear plan of action; waiting for a miracle. We tried to regain our self-esteem, reassess our nationality and renew our faith in humanity. The time spent in these camps gave us an opportunity to regain our health, reflect on our destiny, and meet the personal challenge of recouping our dignity and self-esteem.

We suffered multiple setbacks. The most common problem was lack of physical and mental health. Many of us were confused, debilitated, and unable to deal with daily life situations. We were psychologically and physically shell-shocked.

Most of us were skeletal and severely malnourished. The war was over, but times were not easy. There were typical post-war food shortages throughout Europe. We had no jobs, and lacked funds to buy food, clothes or housing. We needed time to travel in order to search for the remnants of our families. We had no legal documents which would prove our identity and connect us to our parents, to our former homes and properties, even to our former countries.

From 1939 until May of 1945, Hitler's rampage of mass destruction devastated all of Europe and especially the Jews of Europe. The majority of us were not fully aware of the extent of our individual and collective losses until many months, or even years after the war's end.

We were unable to comprehend that six million of Europe's Jews had vanished; entire communities were murdered, and so few of us — less than 10 percent — had survived the murderous German "Final Solution."

World War II was over. But the realization of such a heretofore unheard-of catastrophe — the murder of six million Jews — gave rise to a new word: The "Holocaust."

As for me, those horrifying days between the spring of 1944 and mid-1946 provided a painful personal history. I had suffered in succession forced incarceration in the Beregszász Ghetto, the murder of most of my family in the Auschwitz-Birkenau, Bergen-Belsen and Dachau concentration camps, and eight months in the "Work-to-Death" concentration camp of Jaworzno in Upper Silesia. After the Russian Army liberated me in early 1945, I essentially walked home to Vásárosnamény. When my surviving siblings returned home, I helped to reopen the shattered Zelczer Family Bakery business in Vásárosnamény.

Then, in 1946, just a bit over two years after the Hungarians dragged me into the Ghetto, I had to run away from my place of origin. I left behind our beloved family home and scampered away stealthily from my hometown, like a stranger.

I was dreadfully tired of Europe and wanted to get away from its degenerate culture of hatred and its terrible bloodbaths. After my many traumatic experiences, I was through with Europe and willing to go anywhere.

My first choice was Palestine, the historical Jewish homeland, later to be known as Israel. However, the only way to reach it at that time was to be smuggled in, because the British Government had blocked all road and sea access to the Holy Land. Britain was anxious at all costs to protect its oil supply and safeguard its political interests in the Arab countries.

For Britain, it was a simple decision. The Arabs had oil, were wealthy and influential. The Jews in Palestine had no money, no army, no oil, no influence, and very few friends. In addition, Great Britain did not feel obligated in any way to the post-Holocaust Jews in Palestine.

Britain was openly cruel, callously unjust and deceitful to the Jews living in Israel, as well as to the Jews who survived the Holocaust. It refused to abide by its League of Nations mandate and its own Balfour Declaration, calling for a "national home" for the Jews in Palestine.

For Britain it was a cold political calculation. To help or even permit Jews to regain their historical country was not going to accomplish Britain's immediate oil goals, nor would it help its long-term strategies, whose aim was to maintain its foothold in the Middle East and preserve its Empire.

Britain did all it could to keep Jews from reaching the one place that the world knew to be their historic homeland. In fact, the free world was quite aware that the British Navy detained about 15,000 would-be Jewish immigrants and kept them behind barbed wire fences on the island of Cyprus, rather than allow them to reach Palestine.

There were reliable reports and many rumors that the British Navy torpedoed and sank dozens of small fishing boats and ferryboats crammed with surviving Jews trying to reach Israel who were simply on their way to live in their historic homeland.

My surviving brothers and I: Herman on my left, Mike on my right, and myself in front. Vásárosnamény, Hungary, 1945/ 1946.

Having survived Auschwitz-Birkenau, few of us really wanted to see, much less live inside, another building fenced in with barbed-wire or a detention camp. Once news of Cyprus and its barbed-wire fences reached the Jewish DP camps in Europe, only a small percentage of people were willing to brave the risk of attempting to travel to Israel illegally. The rest of us decided to explore more options until this one became more feasible.

The next alternative was to seek a visa to America, Canada, South America or Australia; however, those options were very difficult to realize.

We lay trapped in the DP camps. We didn't want to go back to the countries that had betrayed us. On the other hand, the world outside was not ready to accept us or let us back into our historic homeland. We had a few good Jewish representatives, but we had no military or the political or financial means to handle our precarious situation. We were powerless.

Survivors stayed in DP camps for many reasons, and each camp contained people of many nationalities and covered a wide range of needs. Based on my own experiences, I will describe the types of camps and the people who populated them.

In addition to Jews, the DP camps contained the following groups of people:

1) GYPSIES, HOMOSEXUALS, SEVENTH DAY ADVENTISTS,
   AND ANTI-FASCISTS

Like Jews, they were victims of German cruelty. Fearing continued discrimination based on their race, religion, sexual orientation, or political beliefs, they felt unsafe returning to their former homes. Each of these groups was but a small minority within their home countries, and they had no confidence that they would not be ostracized — or worse.

2) FORMER "VOLUNTEER FACTORY WORKERS" WHO HAD
   SOUGHT TO HELP GERMANY'S WAR EFFORT

These volunteer Nazi men and women came from an assortment of European countries. Many feared to return home lest the new Communist home government hold them accountable for their past efforts on behalf of Nazi Germany.

3) FORMER SS OFFICERS, GUARDS, UNDERCOVER AGENTS,
   SECRET POLICE, COLLABORATORS, MURDEROUS NAZI
   FUNCTIONARIES, NAZI-ERA JUDGES AND LAW ENFORCERS
   ORIGINATING FROM GERMANY AND AUSTRIA

These SS men feared to return to their hometowns, yet felt safe in the DP camps where they easily obtained and lived with newly created identities, a luxury not easily available to them at home.

Upon receiving their newly registered (= invented) names in the DP camps, many thousands moved to different cities in their home country. Countless numbers disappeared with new identities into South America, Canada and elsewhere. An inestimable number of them immigrated to and melded into the USA.

4) SS VOLUNTEERS AND NAZIS ORIGINATING FROM AREAS THAT CAME UNDER RUSSIAN CONTROL, SUCH AS: EAST GERMANY, POLAND, UKRAINE, HUNGARY, ROMANIA, CZECHOSLOVAKIA AND YUGOSLAVIA

The Nazis from these areas were most afraid to go home — with good reason. They feared severe prosecution in the harsh Communist-oriented courts for the massive number of murders they committed during their brutal and vicious Nazi years. For example, in the vast Bergen Belsen Concentration Camp area alone, about 50,000 Russian POWs were reported to have been starved and murdered by volunteer SS groups and Wehrmacht German Nazi soldiers.

The reason these SS men and their Nazi sympathizers came to settle in these DP camps was that, here, it was easy to invent new identities for themselves. They would falsely claim that the Nazi Germans had taken away their identity papers, when, in fact, they themselves had destroyed their Nazi identification documents and excised their secret SS underarm tattoos that had previously proudly identified them as part of the murderous SS service. Similarly, they skillfully developed false histories of how they got to Germany or Austria and faked new professions there, often taking on the names of formerly decent but now dead citizens.

Survivors' needs in DP Camps*

After liberation, the concentration camp survivors had many urgent needs, such as:

*   Nourishing food, good medicine and rest.

---

* In the DP camps in the American and British Zones of Germany and Austria.

*   Help in organizing and starting the search for surviving family members. The newly-liberated survivors were scattered in many European countries, in a large number of liberated concentration camps, hospitals, nursing homes, and private homes in Sweden, France, Belgium, and in some European countries under Communist Russian rule.

*   Time to deal emotionally with the new realities of life and death, and the horrible loss of parents, children, siblings, uncles, aunts, cousins and friends.

*   An opportunity to forge a new life, learn a new profession or method of earning a living, make up for lost schooling and training, make new friends and, in many instances, get married or re-married.

Searching for relatives was very difficult. We had no access to newspapers, radios or telephones to help us, and even when these services became slowly available, most of us had no money with which to buy them.

Within the DP camps, survivors with similar social, religious or political philosophies tended to congregate and live close to one another. The various Zionist groups, sports groups and religious groups had the opportunity to live in the same or adjacent barracks. Though these areas were heavily crowded and lacked privacy, this was a great psychological support for all.

The United Nations Relief and Rehabilitation Administration, known by its acronym UNRRA, and the International Relief Organization, known as the IRO, gave us a modest amount of non-kosher and kosher food. They also provided a quantity of used clothing, army folding cots for sleep and some essential linen.

The American Jewish Joint Distribution Committee (JDC) and the Hebrew Immigrant Aid Society of New York (HIAS) helped immensely. A few smaller Jewish organizations also provided some free clothing, food and occasional delicacies.

Sporadically, we received cans of sardines or tuna fish, a box of sugar, bars of chocolate and some religious articles.

A limited amount of medical and emergency help was available in the DP camps' infirmaries. If hospitalization was required, the people in charge arranged with a nearby German hospital to handle the patient.

Ever so slowly, we faced reality and started to deal with it. Those of us who were well enough, traveled from camp to camp to seek information about our families and to hear the latest rumors and news of the day or week. We constantly collected information from returning or traveling survivors with snips of information about, or sightings of, a lost wife, husband, father, mother, sibling, cousin, aunt, uncle, classmate, or friend.

Overheard bits of conversation in a lunch room, laundry room or hallway mentioning a recognizable family name were sufficient to raise our hopes and send us running to some faraway DP camp to continue to widen the search for our families.

How Russia dealt with Nazis

Unlike the Americans and the British, the Russians suffered colossal atrocities and carnage at the hands of the Nazi German Army, the Hungarian Army and their Axis allies. Therefore, the Russians dealt severely with former Nazis, their leaders and their collaborators.

In order to understand the Russian actions and feelings following the war, one needs to know the facts. In pure statistics, the Russians suffered the greatest number of human losses from the Nazi-led Axis powers. Most reliable reports state that up to 26 million Russians were killed,* and countless millions more were crippled and wounded for life.

Not only the SS, but also the ordinary German Wehrmacht

---

* http://en.wikipedia.org/wiki/World_War_II_casualties_of_the_Soviet_Union.

Army soldier had no problem with mass-killing Russian civilian men, women, children and babies. We saw some of these dreadful massacre pictures proudly displayed in the Hungarian newspapers prior to our incarceration in the Beregszász Ghetto, and before our own tragic deportation to Auschwitz-Birkenau.

Therefore, during the first six months after WWII, the Russians were ready to take brutal revenge against Nazis wherever they found them, sometime killing them without a trial or other delay. The Russians had their own schedule for a fractional repayment of their enormously tragic and cruel losses. They killed, jailed and punished many Nazis who fell within their reach in the early days after the war.

How the US and Great Britain dealt with Nazis

On the other hand, the American and the British authorities had their own self-serving agenda. Due to their long-standing fear and alarm at the spread of Russian Communism in Europe, as well as beyond, they decided to be lenient with the SS men, Gestapo, German soldiers and even with the Nazi German leadership.

They felt that they could surreptitiously use the well-trained Nazi scientists, engineers, leaders, soldiers and even the entire chastised German nation to bolster the efforts against the spread of Communism. This became their long-term political policy.

This easygoing approach encouraged thousands of SS and other Nazi criminals to claim for themselves the status of "victims of Nazi persecution."

In fact, in the gentile DP camps, anyone could claim to be a Nazi victim. They simply destroyed their Nazi documents and claimed to be victims of Nazi persecution. With newly invented names and new documents, they were ready to travel. Nazis successfully used the DP camp setting in the British and the American zones of Occupied Germany and Austria as vehicles to quietly disappear into Germany, England, South America, Australia, Canada and the United States.

Several clandestine Christian groups and others operated a number of secret escape routes. Organizations called the routes "rat lines" or "rat routes." ODESSA and other groups provided the SS and other Nazi escapees with false papers, a supply of cash and fully paid travel tickets. They successfully planned and funded the escape and resettlement of countless Nazi murderers and their sympathizers into many different countries.

According to reports, there were about 8,000 SS men and women operating the murder camps in Auschwitz-Birkenau alone. Out of these, nearly 90% — about 7,200 — survived the war. Yet in the end, fewer than 800 of them actually faced prosecution.

Let us keep in mind the enormity of their crime. Out of the reported 1,300,000 human beings forcibly delivered to Auschwitz-Birkenau, the Nazis gassed, suffocated and burned 1,100,000 on the day of their arrival.*

Dr. Josef Mengele and Adolph Eichmann are just two examples of the many thousands of SS personnel who successfully disappeared into Argentina** and numerous other countries in South America, the Middle East, and Eastern Europe and even into Western Europe.

Cold-blooded and deceitful organizations aided and abetted their escapes. I still lie awake at night and wonder how they justified themselves to their God — assuming they have one — their people and their families?

---

* If similar patterns are found to have been true in other concentration camps, the oft-quoted number of six million Shoah victims might actually be well more than six million.

** Eichmann was caught by Israeli security agencies in 1960, and was executed in Israel in 1962.

It must be fully recognized that the murderous SS men and women were *not* drafted or forced into the SS service. They were full-fledged volunteers. In fact, every Axis-country citizen was eligible to sign-up for the SS — so long as he/she was certified as being trustworthy by known Nazis.

The legitimate DP groups were deeply distressed that the vast majority of SS personnel successfully evaded justice and easily melted away, disappearing amongst their German, Austrian and other like-minded friends from other countries.

Sadly, except for the top 100 to 200 Nazi leaders, the American and British authorities were willing to overlook the Nazis' murderous past.

In the DP camp, many of us signed up for one of the many courses in tailoring, woodworking and other vocational skills that the Organization for Rehabilitation through Training, known universally as ORT, had so competently organized. Other Jewish groups offered similar help but not on as wide a scale or of such high quality. ORT had well-seasoned professional trainers, while others had mainly politically connected appointees with inferior professional capabilities.

My surviving older siblings found spouses and their healing process started. After a short hiatus, my older brother Mike married Yitti Kleinbart in Pocking, Germany. Within a few months of our return to Vásárosnamény, my sister Helen married Miklós Friedman. My sister Ruci married Sol Lebovits in Leipheim, Germany, and my brother Hershel (Herman) married Feigele (Margaret) Klein in 1948, in Cleveland, Ohio.

The Ernie Pyle

Unexpectedly, a small window of opportunity opened up for me. A tiny number of Certificates of Entry to the United States became available for surviving youth. I registered at once, and was fortunate to make it to America and start a new life.

On July 29, 1947, I boarded the steamship Ernie Pyle in the port city of Bremen (Bremerhaven), Germany; its destination was New York. The ship was named after the famous and beloved American war correspondent Ernie Pyle who was killed in the waning days of World War II. It was a troop-ship that shuttled back and forth between Europe and the United States, ferrying active and discharged soldiers. The ship had three-tiered army bunk beds for its passengers.

Prior to my boarding in Bremerhaven, I received five dollars of spending money for the journey from someone I believe was a JJDC (Jewish Joint Distribution Committee) representative. It is my understanding that it was the JJDC's social agency which arranged the trip for us, helped us get the visas to enter the USA, and made the travel arrangements.

I will never forget my first panoramic view of the Atlantic Ocean. I watched in awe from the top deck as the ship moved gently forward, exposing more and more of the seemingly endless, shimmering sea. At the very same time, the visible land area behind me was leisurely fading and shrinking until it became a small and insignificant smudge on the distant horizon. It was a mesmerizing and breathtaking sight for a youthful and inexperienced sea traveler.

For a short while, I was oblivious to everything and everyone around me. I felt as though I was utterly lost and floating in a large wasteland of water. When I finally came to myself, I recited the specially prescribed blessing, "Blessed are You, Hashem, our God, King of the Universe, Who made the great sea."

The second day on board, I became aware that there were about eight other young Holocaust survivors on the ship. I made friends with two boys and a girl. They all shared my problem regarding the non-kosher food. Like me, they did not eat the delicious-looking, tempting cooked meals served in the ship's dining room. Nevertheless, we did not go hungry.

This was an American ship carrying American soldiers and a wonderful variety of delicious food was available in the kitchen and dining area. There was an ample supply of bread, milk, dry cereals, juices and mouth-watering fruits and vegetables. Among the fruits were some we had never seen, including bananas, papayas, mangos and more.

On the fourth day, while I was seemingly alone on the top deck, I surveyed my surroundings for a second time. As if in a trance, I became keenly aware of the three most colossal physical things visible to me: the enormous golden and glistening summer sun, the giant sea with its nonstop waves endlessly whipping the ship on its sides, and finally, the ship itself, with its military load in its belly and hundreds of passengers on the top layers. However, I very soon realized that the Ernie Pyle was not as large as I had thought, and I now saw it as just a small kayak slowly bobbing atop the horizon-to-horizon sea. Yet, it seemed to know where it was going, moving fearlessly along an unmarked path through the deep and endless waters.

I continued to daydream when suddenly I was startled out of my spell by a blaring announcement on the loudspeaker, inviting everyone to challenge the visiting chess champion in simultaneous games in the dining room. After a moment's thought, I decided to take my turn at this adventure. My single concern was that I would not be able to speak to the champion because my English was very limited and rudimentary.

As I arrived in the dining room, I saw a rectangular arrangement of long narrow tables with about 60 soldiers lined up on its four outer perimeters. I sheepishly pulled up a chair and placed myself in front of one of the prepared chess sets.

To me, it was an Olympian sight to watch the champion chess player slowly walk the inner perimeter from set to set, and knock out most of his opponents, including me, in four to seven moves. Then, he sat down and seriously entertained himself with the few remaining and obviously more experienced challengers. It was fun to observe his moves. Like the proverbial cat playing with a cornered mouse, he slowly but gingerly finished them all off.

After 14 days of relatively smooth summer sailing, our ship arrived at the harbor in New York. On August 11, 1947, I landed in this breathtaking and free country which I deeply love, respect and support.

I soon completed the required pages of paperwork for entry and landing purposes, and a nice tall young man in his 20s presented himself and greeted me with a friendly smile. He carefully and slowly stated that he was from a certain social agency, that he had a train ticket in my name, and that he would accompany me to Cleveland, Ohio. Upon our arrival at the East Cleveland Pennsylvania Railroad Station, he took me straight to a lovely sprawling and tree-lined estate, known as Bellefaire.

Bellefaire: The first step towards rebuilding life

In the summer of 1947, Bellefaire served as an Orthodox Jewish Children's Home for the extended geographic area. Its origins go back to about 1927, when the B'nai B'rith fraternal organization built the orphanage on 32 tree-lined acres in University Heights. The numerous orphans of those days filled it to capacity.

Before its magnificent modern campus was built, the orphanage, known then as The Jewish Orphan Asylum, had been located somewhere on Cleveland's East Side, since its official opening in 1868.

Upon my arrival, the friendly welcoming officer in charge placed me with a group of about 18 young refugee boys who had arrived months ahead of me. We were all Holocaust survivors from various European countries.

The management of Bellefaire appointed Mr. and Mrs. Eric Hershfeld, the well-educated and caring supervisors, as our "cottage parents." They were in charge of our daily activities, provided us with lots of nourishing food from their modern kosher kitchen, and gave us excellent "food for thought," as well. Indeed, the orphanage treated us with tender loving care. The rooms were large, clean, and airy, providing excellent shelter and a peaceful growing environment.

Due to our troubled pre-World War II years, followed by our youthful incarceration in the ghettos and murderous concentration camps, and finally our stay in DP camps in western Germany, we were very much behind in our schooling. It was in Bellefaire that we received our basic American history orientation and laid the foundation for our English-language program.

We all thrived under the direction of two unforgettable and wonderful friends, Drs. May and Charles E. Simon. This husband-and-wife pair crammed into their lectures important issues that we never had the chance to learn in Europe. Their lectures were full of love and concern for our future. Additionally, Dr. Manfred Strauss, a distinguished college professor of mathematics, gave us a "head start" in our math proficiency.

The names of three boys in our group which I still remember are Israel Stark, Jacob Risse and Leon Shear. I spent a memorable month with them at Bellefaire while we acclimated to the abundant freedoms and wonders of America.

A few days before Rosh Hashanah of 1947, I voluntarily left the institution. I joined my brother, Herman, who was boarding on Amor Avenue with the ever-friendly Hartman family. Amor Avenue was one of the many fine residential streets off East 105th street, in what was then one of the primary Jewish neighborhoods of Cleveland.

For Rosh Hashanah and Yom Kippur, we attended holiday services at the Shómer Shabbat Congregation directed by the elderly Rabbi Schwartz. The shul was located on East 105th street, between Superior and St. Clair Avenues. There were many fine old synagogues in the area, including the Columbia

Avenue Synagogue, where the wise and aging Rabbi Dr. Phillip Rosenberg was its gifted leader and multilingual orator.

Life and liberty: The treasured freedoms of America

My first job was of a temporary nature at the Heights Baking Company, located on Coventry Road, near Mayfield. I worked additional day and night shifts in other bakeries in town, such as the Cleveland Grocers Baking Company on Woodland Avenue, Joseph's Bakery on Kinsman Road and several others. Subsequently I worked at Pollack's Bakery on East 105th street. Mr. Pollack and I produced a full line of bakery products, including bread and cakes.

Life was very satisfying. I was able to support myself and save money to send CARE relief packages to my hungry siblings still languishing in the DP camps of Europe. Although I worked long hours, I still made time to go to night school and learn the English language. I listened carefully and sincerely appreciated when friends suggested corrections.

The next year, I found the girl of my dreams, Ruth Kohn. Our similar family backgrounds, life outlook and Holocaust experiences were all contributing elements to our match. Ruth and I married in 1948.

We soon determined that the baking business, which meant having to get up at 3:00 a.m. each morning, was not conducive for a good family life. I decided to start

Spring 1948, Cleveland, Ohio.
My first custom-made suit.

training as an electrician. This move cut my wages in half, but I was determined to learn the electrical trade.

I read library books and talked to building-trades workers whenever the opportunity arose. I spent hours in the home of Mr. Charles Moskovitz where he explained to me the intricacies of the then popular "knob-and-tube" house wiring techniques, commonly used in new house construction in the Greater Cleveland area.

I worked long hours for several small electrical contracting companies until I worked my way up and learned the trade. Later on, I worked at the Erie Electric Co. After a while, the owner, Mr. Everett Rosen, put me in charge of training his new employees in electrical wiring for homes and stores.

Around 1956, Ruth and I decided to go into the electrical contracting business. She became the secretary and bookkeeper and did the ordering of the electrical supplies. I went out to search for work, picked up supplies at the wholesaler and completed the electrical installation work myself. As time went on, our customers were pleased and our work base expanded. The hours were long but rewarding. We reinvested and risked our earnings to make growth possible.

We hired several employees and built a fine electrical business. We kept very busy, improved the life of our employees, our children, and ourselves, and gave charity to various organizations.

Having my basic human freedoms torn from me by ruthless and malicious governments, I am forever grateful for all the wonderful opportunities this great democratic country provides and will forever treasure the liberties guaranteed under its wise and protective constitution.

❧ 5 ❧
My Reflections

Christian anti-Semitism

On October 5, 1999, at a Cleveland Jewish Community Center event sponsored by the Cleveland Chapter of the American Jewish Committee, a Catholic Priest, Rev. John Pawlikowsky, declared:* "The Christian tradition of anti-Semitism was not marginal to attitudes of church piety. They were central."

I deeply appreciated Rev. Pawlikowsky's forthright honesty and courage. This was indeed a great revelation to a large segment of the American public, but his poignant remark was not news to those of us who had survived the Holocaust, whose families had felt the anti-Semitic tragedy personally, and who had suffered from the ongoing and well-planned anti-Semitism of church teachings.

Since the conversion to Christianity of the Roman Emperor Constantine about 1,700 years ago, churchgoers have been taught by their spiritual mentors to hate, despise, rob, and even kill Jews. Indeed, throughout much of their history, both the Christian Church as such and its believers as individuals often did precisely that. Their religion wrongly taught them that Jews killed their god.

I still remember that in the mandatory public school religious hour lessons back in Hungary, they derogatorily called us "Jews, the Christ Killers," adding, "Jew... go to Palestine!" for good measure.

---

* As quoted in *The Cleveland Jewish News*.

Introduction to hatred

Hungarian law mandated the teaching of religion in all public schools throughout the country. In my hometown, Vásáros-namény, the Roman Catholic and the Reformed Catholic priests came to the public school to teach their particular denomination's interpretation of the Bible. Between themselves, they may have had minor or even major differences on many Biblical or religious interpretations, but they both agreed on one point: the prerequisite to provoke and ingrain anti-Semitism.

Their religious teachings actively fostered bigotry, intolerance, arrogance and beatings. They regularly and openly taught students that the Jews killed their "God," that we are part of the "Antichrist," and that they are therefore obligated to hate, beat and punish Jews. Many a time, following religious classes, the Christian children would beat us up, taunt, spit and curse us on the way home from school. From 1939 and up to our Ghettoization, Jewish children frequently came home with bruised bodies and bloody noses.

To ensure that Jewish boys and girls would not have to attend the Catechism classes and be forced to listen to anti-Jewish lectures by the priests, our Rabbi Kohn came to public school each week to teach Jewish religious classes at the same hours as the priests. Rabbi Kohn kept his lectures religiously neutral, repeatedly teaching us about Adam and Eve, Noah's Ark, and other noncontroversial Bible stories.

The public school rules forbade Rabbi Kohn from using Hebrew, so he conducted his lectures in Hungarian. His religious classes worked well for us because they were very basic and easy, involving mostly stories.

However, on days when Rabbi Kohn was unable to teach, we had a big problem. On those occasions, we had to attend the priest's religious classes, listen to his anti-Jewish tirades, kneel down and say the Christian prayers and listen to Catechism lectures. It was indeed difficult to sit through those classes where we heard the repeated teachings of intolerance, bigotry and detestation. Unfortunately, the teaching of hatred was extremely pervasive and successful.

Jews hiding among Christians

From about 1941 to early 1944, a small portion of Hungarian Jews took flight. They simply disappeared. Typically, they were single men or women, young children sent away by desperate parents, or small, mobile families. Hungarian politics and foreign policy had become increasingly pro-Fascist and pro-Nazi, and some Jews became alert, concerned, and distrustful of the government. Those with a daring nature who were willing to act on scant information and fuzzy rumors were determined to save themselves.

Various people dealt with this seemingly impending crisis in the following ways:

* A small number ran away to Budapest or far-off locations where they essentially shed their Jewishness. They purchased Christian/Aryan identity papers, discarded their Jewish clothes, attended church regularly, and by and large, blended into the general population.
* Some paid exorbitant bribes or begged their way into existing hiding places.
* Others, with the help of respectable and caring Gentiles, went into hiding in bunkers, haylofts, barns, clandestinely-built concealed rooms and false attics. Usually, someone promised to sustain them with food on a daily or weekly basis, and was paid for the food accordingly.
* A number joined lonely, out-of-the-way farms where they became free farmhands or farm-maids in complete isolation.

My Uncle Baruch took advantage of a rare opportunity to run away from his closely guarded jail cell. The police in Budapest had moved him into a second-story prison cell. From there, it was certain he would be deported to a concentration camp. One day, Uncle Baruch broke the window bar and jumped out to the ground below.

Through the so-called "grapevine," he made contact with friends and acquired the false identity papers of a gentile. With his beard shaved off and dressed like a gentile, he worked as a professional Christian baker in the well-known Weisz Bakery and elsewhere in Budapest. He managed to survive the war. But, his wife and children didn't fare as well. The Hungarians forced his wife and most of his children into a ghetto. They were then shipped in cattle boxcars to Auschwitz-Birkenau and other concentration camps, where his wife and some of their children were murdered.

Around 1943, my older brother, Mike, who was about 27 at the time, moved to Budapest. He bought Christian papers and registered as a gentile citizen. He worked as a master baker at the Weisz Bakery and other bakeries in the Budapest area. He often changed jobs from one bakery to another in order to avoid recognition or suspicion of being a Jew.

In wartime Hungary, Jews were not allowed to obtain work permits and therefore could not earn any money nor receive any ration tickets. Consequently, they could not buy or obtain food. In this fashion, the Hungarian government planned to starve the Jews.

In stepped my brother, Mike, who had the proverbial "warm and soft heart" and was always keenly conscious of the pain of others. He went out of his way to help anyone, even at the greatest personal risk. Mike used most of his salary to buy bread illegally at the bakery where he worked and gave it away free to the ill-fated Jews who were hiding with no false papers, no food ration tickets and no money.

Unfortunately, after many months of successful charitable accomplishments, the Hungarian Arrowhead Nazis caught him while he was on one of his bread delivery missions to starving Jews who were hiding in a basement. The Nazis took away his precious load of bread, beat him up severely, jailed him, and then deported him to the infamous Mauthausen Concentration Camp in Austria. He did survive the Holocaust.

Surtcha Schwartz (née Beilush), my mother's first cousin from Nyirbátor, was one of those who suddenly disappeared. She and her two young daughters, Erica and Maca fled to the city of Nagyvárad, and from there, they escaped to Budapest. They managed to hide behind false Christian papers. The girls were about 14 and 16 years old, and they worked at various jobs.

Surtcha and her two daughters survived the war. However, the Germans and Hungarians murdered her two sons, her parents, and six pairs of her married siblings including all their young children.

For strong-minded singles and small families with some cash, it was possible to hide successfully. But if a large family wished to stay together and hide, they faced nearly insurmountable problems: It was next to impossible for a large family to obtain sufficient Aryan papers, an adequate food supply, a large enough hiding location, and sufficient cash and valuables to tide them over.

Jewish parents' dilemma

"Should I buy Gentile ID papers?"

Desperate, daring and well-to-do parents with valuables or cash, who sought to escape from the ghetto, had to find a way to complete the following perplexing undertakings:

1) Find a reliable outside contact to buy gentile identity papers for the entire family.

2) Smuggle the family out of the Ghetto with bribes or other well-paid outside assistance.

3) Find means of travel by bus, train, or horse-and-wagon for the whole family, while avoiding detection as a run-away Jewish family. Prepare the family for night travel in order to pass through towns along the planned escape route without attracting the attention of police or hostile citizens.

4) Locate and arrange for a friendly gentile place to hide along the escape route. By 1944, the majority of Jews were captives in Ghettos throughout Hungary, and there was no possibility of availing oneself of Jewish hospitality.

5) Locate a friendly border-town — i.e., with residents open to bribes — near Romania or Yugoslavia. These two countries were the only realistic options at this time.

6) Teach one's children several languages to be able to converse with the gendararmes if they were to stop them on the escape route — either while walking, on a bus, on a train, in a taxi, or aboard a hired horse-wagon.

7) Find a reliable gentile to smuggle the family across the border — one that would not turn them over to the gendarmes. 70% of the fee was usually paid in advance and 30% "upon delivery."

8) Purchase false passports for the whole family to match

newly-created Aryan/Christian birth certificates or other acceptable identity papers.

9) Buy two sets of false papers: a Hungarian set to provide cover while travelling to a border town, and a foreign set for use after crossing over to a "safe country."

10) Prepare the family to learn the language of their new host country.

11) Prepare sufficient local and foreign currency, including diamonds and gold for the smugglers and for any additional bribes needed along the escape route, keeping in mind that the mere possession of foreign currency was a highly punishable crime in Hungary.

Throughout the preparations, one question was constantly in the foreground. "Where will my family be more at risk: trying to avoid capture by the gendarmes along our escape route, or remaining within the confines of the Ghetto with thousands of other Jews?"

For the vast majority of captives inside the Ghetto, an escape plan of this nature was not realistic because:

1) the amount of cash and jewelry needed for bribes to get out of the Ghetto was prohibitive.

2) to purchase false identity papers was costly.

3) to find a safe place was beyond the capabilities of most Ghetto inmates.

4) finally, the Ghetto dwellers often reasoned that "there is safety in numbers," and they were better off staying with a large group rather than going on their own.

Ghettos compared:
Original ghettos and later ghettos

The word "Ghetto" resonates sadly for many Jewish people. To the newly initiated in history, it is perhaps suggestive of the old

Jewish Diaspora. However, there are basic differences in the ghettos where our ancestors were forced to live, and those of the Hitler era.

In the ghettos of our ancestors, Jews were restricted and tightly crammed into strictly allotted neighborhoods in or outside cities and towns. Characteristically, they lived with their extended families in fear and under difficult conditions and were heavily taxed. In most cases, Jews were restricted in their choice of profession and clientele, sometimes forced to deal only with their ghetto brethren. They lived under these miserable physical conditions for hundreds of years.

Every so often, the government, the church, the potentate or the baron expelled them and their families into the wilderness or into neighboring countries with meager food and clothing. Over the course of some 300 years, tens of thousands of Jews were killed and maimed in anti-Semitic attacks in the old ghettos.

The Hitler-era ghettos were quite different: They were brutal mass holding cells for Jews of all ages and physical conditions, until they could be transported to mass-murder and slave-labor camps.

In writing the above, it is not my intention to minimize the horrible and murderous conditions suffered by our ancestors in the old ghettos of Europe. Nor do I forgive the perpetrators of the Pogroms, Crusades, Expulsions and Oppressions of our ancestors. Rather, I wish to clearly compare the old "Ghetto," with the similar-sounding Nazi-mandated "Ghetto," and demonstrate that it was a totally different Ghetto.

What was the big difference between them?

The European Ghettos of my youth, from 1938 to 1944, were the result of highly concentrated massive hate-training, prejudice and scapegoating, combined with the buildup of modern mass-killing equipment. The result was the colossal murder of six million Jews in the course of a short six to seven year period.

The ghettos of old never had such ghastly conclusion.

That is the big difference!

Denial and desperate hope

In retrospect, it is quite clear that from 1938/1939, the Jews of Hungary, Czechoslovakia and Romania lived in denial. It seems that our leaders felt that if they would not acknowledge the trouble so obviously brewing on our immediate horizon the problems would go away.

Our Jewish leaders obviously knew about the various anti-Semitic reports from 1939 through 1943, and about the deportation of 60,000 Slovakian Jews to the killing fields of Germany, Poland and the Ukraine. Yet, these reports were utterly silenced — disregarded! False hopes and hallucination were the diet fed to the Jewish public.

Indeed, as late as 1944 and up to the day of deportation, Jews in Hungarian towns and villages simply refused to believe, let alone anticipate the worst.

Our Jewish leaders, civic as well as religious, continued to delude themselves and their members even as late as 1944 when the Hungarians were forcing us into the ghettos. Despite the terrible stories that we heard from Russia, Ukraine, Poland, Germany, Austria, Holland, France and elsewhere, our leadership failed to face reality. They somehow pretended that the mass destruction of our people was not happening* and could not happen. They chose instead to live in denial and ignorant bliss.

Our leaders were well grounded in matters of *Halakhah* (Jewish religious law), but they were politically inexperienced,

---

* See *Min Hameitzar*, by Michael Bear Weismandel, pp. 105-106. Emunah Publishing 1960, 2nd edition.

utterly naïve and quite simply — incompetent. They were seeking mystical meanings to straightforward, openly-declared physical threats from our mortal enemies.

With the passage of time, the option of legal or illegal immigration to Israel or to the Americas became increasingly slim. It is clear that our leaders did not understand the immediate survival needs of the Jewish families. The Nazis were gaining tighter control on our lives as each day passed, and made it more difficult for us to escape Europe.

It pains me to say that the collective paralysis of both religious and lay leadership was unforgivable. They seem to have existed in such a state of denial that their minds failed to register the clear and obvious threats emanating from our enemies.

Many were relying on mystical stories to the willful exclusion of facts in the real world around us. They continued to cling to their illusion that wishing and dreaming would disperse the gathering storm clouds and that our communities would somehow survive.*

Around 1941/1942, the Slovak, Czech, Romanian, and Hungarian Jews became aware of the mass killings in Ukraine, Lithuania, Russia, and Poland. A tiny number of successful runaways secretly reported to Jewish leaders the mass murders which were taking place in Czechoslovakia, Romania, and Hungary.**

For instance, the Bobover Rebbe's brother was successful in escaping from Poland and finally made his way back to Hungary. However, "when he related to officials what he had witnessed, he was forcibly stopped and..."***

Additionally, Mr. Vrba and Mr. Wetzler and a number of others who escaped from Auschwitz-Birkenau warned and

---

* See Braham, Randolph L. with Scott Miller, *The Nazis' Last Victims*, pp. 179, 180, Wayne State University, 1998.

** See *Min Hameitzar*, Hebrew Edition, 1960, Emunah Publishing, pp. 16, 24, 186.

*** See Rafael Grosz, *Our Miraculous Survival*, p. 72, Grosz Brothers Publishing 1997.

briefed the Jewish professional and religious leadership about the ongoing German murders and the continuing destruction of Jewish life. They provided abundant and substantive information.

The Jewish leadership, individually and collectively, failed in their responsibilities. They kept quiet about solid information presented to them and failed to advise the Jewish population. They did not tell them of the grave dangers that were looming. Our leaders lacked good judgment, and they missed opportunities.

In their defense, I must say that they had never been trained in dealing with such monstrous threats as those facing us. With their limited knowledge of world affairs, they tried to lead a broken people who were living among a vicious population. They were not up to such a task. It is also fair to say that they likely felt that issuing grave warnings without providing concrete solutions could cause chaos and panic.

Perhaps, too, as Rabbi Yisachar Teichtal wrote: Our leaders were reluctant to give up their authorized jobs and prestigious rabbinic positions. If people left Europe en-masse, that could jeopardize their families' livelihood in the old European cities and towns. Maybe they were not willing to uproot their own families.*

The sad, final result was that the Hungarians forced all Jews of Bereg County, of which Vásárosnamény was an important part, into the Beregszász Ghetto. The same tragedy recurred in the 34 other horrible ghettos that the Hungarian government strategically located throughout the country.

The lay and religious leaders' behavior resembled that of a group of ostriches hiding their heads in the sand as the predator approaches. They became experts at self-deception and willful deafness.

---

*   See Y. S. Teichtal, *Eim Habanim Semeichah*, Eng. ed., Kol Mevaser Publications, pp. 49 and 319, and Michael Ber Weismandel, *Min Hameitzar*, 2nd ed., p. 151, Emunah Publishing, 1960

Consequently, with the exception of the mostly well-off 1.684 Jews who left with Rezsö Kastner's train to "Palestine," the Jewish community paid a bitter and ultimate price for their leaders' ineptitude.

Wrapping up, as I reflect on my experiences during my teenage incarceration in Auschwitz-Birkenau and the Jaworzno concentration camps, I realize that I, too, repeatedly used psychological self-denial and willful deafness to provide some level of comfort. I anesthetized myself against the ongoing stress and unmitigated pain. The numbness I created via my denial germinated some wiggle-room for desperate hope.

However, the legally responsible and ethically liable communal and religious leaders of European Jewry were 'hired grown-ups,' and they held trusted communal leadership positions. They were not ... teenagers.

Promotion — profit — prestige

Where was the Church? The Church had two agendas: promoting itself and indoctrinating citizens with anti-Semitism and hatred. Powerful and profitable partnerships were formed between Church leaders and various temporal leaders. The boundaries of Church and State became so deeply intermingled that in many countries it was impossible to determine where one began and the other ended. It was what the business world calls a "win-win" situation for both parties.

This cozy amalgamation provided the rulers of both Church and State with a steady flow of cash in the form of mutually approved taxation of the public at large. Additionally, it was common practice to impose more and higher taxes on Jews — including marriage and border-crossing levies.*

It was sadly characteristic throughout Europe that Jews

---

* See: Raphael Patai, *The Jews of Hungary*, pp. 62,63,73,79,85, Wayne State Univ Press, 1996.

would be driven out of a country, and then be readmitted after payment of additional taxes and penalties to various officials and their partners. Furthermore, during the Jews' absence from the country, the Church, the government and neighbors often confiscated their communal and private properties.

This comfortable partnership also required and readily received an abundant flow of blessings, magnanimous praise, and public recognition by Church and State rulers for each other.

The government created new laws that did not recognize minority religions, thus forcing Seventh Day Adventists, Jews, Gypsies, pagans and atheists to pay taxes to the Church.

The kings, nobles and the Church did as they wished. Over the years, the knights of Europe forcibly converted millions of pagans, Jews, Gypsies and other minorities to Christianity. Those who would not convert were often murdered in crusades, inquisitions, pogroms and burnings at the stake in the name of the Holy Roman Empire and the Church. Moreover, "they treated the Jews as human chattel, with whom and to whom these powers could do whatever they wanted."*

The tacit agreement between the two powers was one of solid support for each other. With a few historical exceptions, this union worked well for both, and the synergy of profit and prestige transformed this alliance into an all-powerful entity that knew no boundaries. However, it was most often a deadly disadvantage for all minority religions and non-believers. Due to the Jewish requirement to keep the Sabbath and eat kosher food, which made the Jew conspicuous, life was especially difficult for the Jews.

At times, the public became angry at the licentious, luxurious and wasteful lifestyles of a given head of State or Church. But, a well-timed public statement of praise, of each for the other, tended to pacify or scare off the dissenting public.

---

* Patai, ibid., p. 14.

The Church establishment had acquired the world's largest private real estate empire, consisting of important and prestigiously located buildings and vast land holdings. It also acquired worldwide business operations, cash, broad political recognition and the prestige that goes with all of the above.

The uncontested powers of the Church effectively blinded it to the very basic dictates of its religion, such as Leviticus 19:18, "Love your neighbor as yourself," and the oft-quoted Matthew 5:39, "But I say unto you, that ye resist no evil: but whosoever shall smite thee on thy right cheek, turn to him the other also."

Our ancestors lived under capricious governments that maintained close connections with the anti-Semitic hate teachings of the Church. Together, they created utterly venomous mental images of the Jew.

Today, we clearly understand that these persistent bigoted teachings sparked deep enmity against Jews. In turn, this resulted in pogroms, murders, book-burnings, crusades, inquisitions, expulsions, and ultimately — the Holocaust.

The long and precarious exile

For nearly 2,000 years — since the Romans expelled the Jews and barred them from their land of Israel — the Jews were upstanding, tax-paying citizens in the many countries they lived in. These countries were homeland to many generations of Jews, over many hundreds of years. In many countries, the Jews were invited and warmly received for their craftsmanship skills. In others, their expertise was sought to develop and organize banking and commerce, and often, to help settle vast vacant areas.

Various host countries successfully used Jewish political skills to great advantage. Over the years, some countries openly acknowledged their appreciation for their Jews' loyalty and fine accomplishments. Let us note the Golden Age of Spanish Jewry, as well as the latter years of Franz Josef, the last Emperor of the Austro-Hungarian Empire, where Jews served willingly and valiantly in all areas of military service of the country and in scores of advisory and civilian services. Indeed, many thousands gave their very lives in the process.*

For short periods, when it suited their economic needs, some European countries, such as Germany, Poland, France, and even some Arab countries, treated their Jewish citizens benevolently. However, there was never any guarantee, and the facts that they were loyal and tax-paying citizens for centuries, were born and raised in their countries for generations, had been invited into the countries and did great things for their countries did not prevent their governments, their fellow citizens, and their former good neighbors from turning against them.

Religious fervor, as well as internal or external politics, often provided the spark for the removal of the Jews' freedom, their property and their funds. The governments frequently passed new anti-Jewish laws or renewed some of the old, forgotten ones.

Whether by law or by sheer lawlessness, the reality became such that the Jew's home, business, land, money, and even his very life were all easy prey for kings, judges, princes, dukes, barons, bishops, and local citizens. They readily overlooked the murder of one Jew or 100 Jews.

Historically, this has happened persistently to the people that had no country to call their own. Their members were invited in and welcomed when they were needed, but were then discarded, expelled and destroyed when the job was finished and they were no longer perceived to be useful or needed.

It usually took a volatile mixture of politics, jealousy and

---

* See Y.Y. Greenwald, *A Thousand Years of Jewish Life in Hungary*, pp. 8-12, Parish Press, NY, 1945; and Raphael Patai, *The Jews of Hungary*, pp. 314, 315, 317, etc., Wayne State Univ. Press, Detroit.

religion to fan the burning hatred. The base was the intolerance, bigotry, hatred, racism and violence preached by the
politicians and Churches. The public, the police and the army
would then take their cue and beat, loot, burn and kill Jews.

There would likely have never been a "Jewish Problem" to
resolve, had not the 1,700 years of adamant anti-Semitic
teachings of Constantine I, the first Christian Roman Emperor,
initiated it.

Historians tell us that ever since the destruction of the Second Temple in Jerusalem, the Jew's life in the Diaspora has
been precarious because the Jew was an easily identified minority. He was singled out, harassed and abused at will by his
baron, his bishop, his neighbor or his government. One also
needs to add the profit enhancer. If they drove the Jew out of
the country or killed him, his property was transferred to his
neighbors, his town and his government.

It was easy to select Jews as scapegoats because they were
religiously different. They were a minority and did not belong
to one of the powerful Christian denominations.

Alas, it took little to arouse the new Haman, under a different name in each generation, to do with our Jewish ancestors
as he willed. The Jews were easily discarded, their citizenship
was readily revoked and their lives were effortlessly shattered.
In the 1930s and 40s, ethnic demagoguery was a powerful tool
in the hands of the German Devil and his lackeys.

We suffered a multitude of indignities beyond description.
In country after country, physical, religious and economic harassment of Jews never seemed to cease.*

Jews are an ancient people and have a long national
history beginning with the Exodus from ancient Egypt over
3,300 years ago. Never throughout this amazingly long period
have we lost as many innocent and blameless people as in the
seven-year period of the Holocaust.

---

* See Y. S. Teichtal, *Eim Habanim Semeichah*, p. 335, Kol Mevaser Publishers, 2000).

During the Hitler era, the Nazi educators and instructors of hatred succeeded in creating their own false world via constant repetition of prejudicial fabrications of news and indoctrinating lies. The inculcation of anti-Semitism flowed freely from every type of available media, day and night.

History has a long record of the human capability to perform extreme actions for good and for evil. However, a pinnacle is reached when an entire nation uses its collective invincibility, based on a combination of police and state actions, with local pogroms motivated by the opportunity for systematic looting and open thievery. Unimaginable brutality is the direct result.

In the so-called "civilized" German nation and its enthusiastic Axis allies, poisonous and permanent damage was the natural result of repeated anti-Semitic writings, vile cartoons and hate speeches. Their victims included anyone they considered inferior, members of the "wrong" religion, or any human they deemed, in their bloodthirsty and distorted political doctrine, unworthy of life.

History must never forget what the Germans and their eager partners, the Hungarians, Poles, Slovaks, Romanians, Ukrainians, and Yugoslavs, did to the Jewish people and to the world. It is fundamentally important for the world to read about the bestial behavior of these white-gloved monsters, and to know of their unspeakable atrocities committed during the most brutal seven-year period of human history.

I present my personal experiences as a warning that teaching hate, preaching intolerance, encouraging bigotry and fanaticism will destroy every civilized person's dream of a peaceful and more reasonable world.

Relentless pursuit

Starting from about 1939, our enemies robbed my young generation of our teenage years and took away every bit of our human dignity. Never since the Jews became a people have they experienced as savage an epoch as this one — not even during the 400 years of slavery our ancestors endured in Egypt.

How did our enemies accomplish this?

It started with the Hungarian media, press and radio and was joined by the Hungarian law chambers. They repeatedly emphasized ethnic prejudice and inflamed Jewish scapegoating. Since Jews were in a minority position and did not have the protection of the Church, they automatically became the major victim. The perpetually working propaganda machinery continually produced hateful lies which were successful in demeaning us.

At first, they painted us as the arch-enemy of the State, accusing us of being the cause of food shortages, unemployment, inflation and worldwide political problems. The alleged powers of damage and destruction ascribed to the Jew were skillfully created lies, by a politically strong and spiteful majority population.

The government effortlessly passed new restrictions that unabashedly robbed us of our rights as citizens to retain State licenses, keep our jobs, and earn wages that would feed and clothe our families.

The next step was to confiscate our homes, our farms, our businesses and our religious institutions. Eventually, they also appropriated for themselves our jewelry, money, clothing, furniture, animals, tools of our trade and all other belongings.

Finally, the German government conspired with eager collaborators from other countries of Europe, including the Hungarians, and some of the Moslem lands, to mercilessly slaughter us.

They beat to death, shot, drowned, burned, choked and buried alive millions. When their methods proved too slow and "inefficient" for their planned "Final Solution," they resorted to a novel "industrial" method of killing — mass-gassing and cremation — and murdered the vast majority of our families.

Additionally, in order to make money out of Jewish labor, the Nazis and their civilian and political collaborators selected a small percentage of healthy-looking men and women, whom they felt were fit for hard labor, and brutally enslaved us.

Actually, slavery is not the right word for that, because a smart slave owner feeds his slaves and their families. For good and sound business reasons, the slave-master generally provides his chattel with clothes to protect them from the sun, rain, snow and ice. He makes his slaves work hard and often abuses them, but in the long run, the slave owner makes sure that they have reasonably healthy and long lives. He certainly would not wantonly kill or destroy them.

The Germans and their eager collaborators and war partners were quite different. They forced their Jewish slaves to produce, under sub-human conditions, an assortment of civilian and military products for their war efforts and their civilian populations' needs. Moreover, they essentially starved them with the ultimate intention of killing them all. They thus simultaneously worked and starved them to death.

Beyond a doubt, the carnage that occurred between the years of 1939 through 1945 saw the largest number of Jews ever murdered in such a time span. My direct and immediate ancestors, as well as my nearest and dearest, were among the six million innocent Jews that the Nazis and similar anti-Semites annihilated. The beastly slaughter included 1.5 million children.

Unfortunately, Germany's WW II lasted seven long years. No doubt, the German nation holds the world record of taking the most human lives since the beginning of recorded time. The mad hatred of Germany and its Axis partners — Japan, Hungary, Italy, Romania, Slovakia, Bosnia-Herzegovina, Croatia, and Bulgaria — devoured a reported 55-60 million people.

According to writer Harrison E. Salisbury,* 40 million people were killed on the Russian front alone. Additionally, this extended period of unfathomable human misery and war caused untold billions of dollars in direct financial losses and damage even in 1945 dollar value.

Youthful recollections

Although I was already a mid-teenager and had been helping out in the family business for some time, my life education had really begun in the ghetto of Beregszász at the hands of brutal Hungarian gendarmes. The Hungarian gendarmes had five types of weapons — long guns with mounted bayonets, handguns, leaded-end bludgeons, snarling German shepherd dogs and years of martial training. And I had ... nothing.

They gleefully delivered us into the hands of German and Ukrainian SS military authorities, their mighty officers, and despicable experimentation doctors who slaughtered us in many gruesome ways.

I was only 16½ years old when I arrived at Auschwitz-Birkenau. While I had gained some street smarts during the harsh anti-Semitic life we endured in Vásárosnamény just prior to the war, it was in the malicious jungle of the concentration camp that I began to awaken and understand life intellectually and practically. The painful life-lessons I learned there first-hand were unwritten and frequently unspoken. Most of the learning came by way of brutality, bestial floggings and a denigrating existence. These lessons were simplistic, crude and humiliating.

Upon my arrival at the concentration camp, I found a wide variety of captives. Among them were former day laborers, farmers and owners of stores, large and small. Others were cattle-traders, tradesmen, rabbis, lawyers, pharmacists,

---

* In his book *The Unknown War*, Bantam Books, NY. 1978.

executives, peddlers, doctors, tailors, students, public and parochial school teachers, glazers, professors, accountants and even a few millionaires.

And all were just as powerless, feeble, pathetic and expendable skeleton-like humans as I.

Sarcastic note to the International Red Cross

One might reasonably conclude that from 1939 until the end of World War II, in May of 1945, the ever-so-noble International Red Cross was on an extended vacation — possibly high up in the Alps. I certainly saw none of its representatives in Auschwitz-Birkenau or in the Jaworzno Concentration Camps.

A bit of Red Cross diligence could have easily uncovered that the Germans were unlawfully imprisoning large numbers of Allied soldiers in the German concentration camps.

The imprisonment of captured Allied soldiers in concentration camps was in open contravention of the Geneva Convention rules of war — of which Germany was a signatory — and thus was unlawful.

The Red Cross could have tried to have the captured Allied soldiers transferred to lawful POW camps which were run in accordance with Geneva Convention rules.

Sadly, most of the captured soldiers whom the Germans incarcerated in various concentration camps perished along with the Jews, under cruel and subhuman conditions.

How does one Kill a God?

For a long time, Jews (not the Romans) were regularly accused of killing Jesus, the God, Messiah, and Redeemer of Christendom. This was a most important issue, and in time became a popular belief, particularly among the plain stratum of the

Christian populations.

During my school days, religious instruction in public school was a part of the government-mandated subjects. On rare occasions when our Rabbi was unable to be at school to teach us, Jewish students were ordered to attend the catechism classes taught by the Priest, where we were often vilified and degraded by Christian students, who yelled at us, "you killed our God!"

This open accusation led to widespread anti-Semitism and to violent outbursts against Jews, accusing us to be the "Christ Killers."

I herewith pose the following questions:

Is any man, or a group of men, strong enough to kill a deity? Is the act of killing a Deity accomplished by drowning, with a knife, with an axe, with a sword, with a rope, with incantations, with poisonous snakes, by crucifixion, with gossip, with gunpowder, with anthrax, or with an atom bomb?

Irony aside, we actually need not answer any of the above juvenile questions, because the idea of killing a deity would be insulting and ridiculous to the intelligence of any thoughtful and believing person.

It would not surprise me to learn that Church leaders were fully aware of the falsehood of these charges. Nevertheless, they apparently needed this anti-Semitic hate-story for the brainwashing they practiced on the world's population.

This dishonesty worked very well for international religious promotion, for general political growth, and for the perpetual growth of the Church's extended financial and real estate operations.

On the other hand, I am grateful that a widening circle of Christians has finally begun to confront and rectify their problematic history, especially vis-à-vis the Jews, and have had considerable success in correcting these erroneous and inciteful teaching.

Rational thoughts:
A Survivor's Observations,
Insights, and Lessons

For the most part, the sources of these collected life observations are unknown to me. If you know the source of one or more, please advise me, as it will be my pleasure and duty to give proper credit. The insights noted "(az)" I believe are my own.

■ Governmental permission (as seen in Germany, Austria, Hungary, Poland, Ukraine, Czechoslovakia, France, Greece, etc.) to plunder a Jewish neighbor and take his house, business, license, farmland and personal belongings must have been very difficult to resist — even for good neighbors and otherwise excellent citizens. (az)

■ With indoctrination of hate, bigotry and prejudice, a good neighbor can be led to become mute, blind, deaf, and dumb or any combination thereof. (az)

■ To have a grasp of the future, one must comprehend the past.

■ Prejudice and intolerance, as promulgated by the Mullahs, are dangerous to the life of every non-Muslim.

■ The naiveté of a large assortment of leaders continues to be unmistakably demonstrated when they fail to believe the clearly announced threats of their sworn enemies. (az)

- Keep your eyes and ears to the ground, and your heart and hopes to the sky. (Talmud, Yevamot, p. 105b)

- Vigilance against evil must be a top priority of every human — at all times.

- The combination of inexperience, know-it-all attitude, foggy and selfish thinking and errors of judgment by Jewish leadership proved to be deadly to millions. (az)

- With a newly-learned dose of prejudice and discrimination, even a seemingly "neutral" neighbor may turn against you.

- After the terrible Shoah, we must learn to be practical, pragmatic, and realistic, and avoid prominent well-meaning leaders who end up betraying us.

- Hitler's search for a scapegoat for WW I, plus the unprotected minority position of the Jew, were key elements in breeding the Holocaust. (az)

- In times of trouble, large cities are generally safer than small ones as they are more likely to offer reliable information and additional options for "action." (az)

- Every Jew must be eternally vigilant against any form of deception and not rely on misguided and half-baked information — whatever its source. (az)

- The human psyche has many dark corners.

- Given proper inducements, a government that is friendly to Jews today is liable to abandon, deceive and turn against them within a fortnight.

- Misleading the public can be quite easy when the listeners do not have all the facts.

- If the past is an indication of the future — then welcome to the future.

- Some people can be fooled some of the time — only fools can be fooled all the time.

- Choose your leaders with care. From 1929 to 1944 life in Europe became increasingly more dangerous for Jews. Certain alluring loud and persuasive leaders directed the Orthodox community. Only when their own lives turned out to be in danger were they willing to understand the gravity of the situation. At that point, they quickly disappeared and managed to find a safety train to Palestine while leaving the misguided behind. (az)

- The Ostrich Solution — "If I pretend not to see the problem, the problem will go away" might work for ostriches... but not for human beings. (az)

- There is no boundary to the human mind's capacity to deceive its very owner.

- In the long run, we may not have the ability to stop anti-Semitism, but with our continued strong support, we can ease the pain of our brothers and sisters in Israel and in countries around the world.

- Do not assign to strangers the responsibility for decisions that are rightfully yours. You and you alone are your most reliable final advisor.

- We must support Israel emotionally, politically and financially — with our hearts, with our influence, with our affluence and with our prayers.

- The immense power of propaganda must never be underestimated.

- Memories can be a bit short-term and are prone to simple and selfish re-interpretation.

- Be aware of your political surroundings as the very safety of your family may depend on it.

- The deep-seated tradition of *"Gam zeh ya'avor"* ("This too shall pass") often prevailed before and during World War II — to the terrible detriment of countless victims.

- When pressure and turmoil increased, some leaders chose their own survival first. (az)

- Just because leaders issue pronouncements, it does not mean that you have to roll over, park your brain and play dead.

- Traditionally, so-called "small leaders" are coerced into teamwork by the know-it-all, so-called "Big Leaders."

- In the world of foreign politics and affairs of state, our leaders were recurrently naïve men of undersized vision and deprived sight.

- Historically, the offer of "free Jewish property for the taking" has always been an enticing promise for an attack on the Jewish minority. (az)

- Don't park your brain on the street just because you went inside to listen to an opinion.

- It is good to keep an open mind, but do not let your brains fall out. (Dr. Joan Borysenko, Ph.D.)

- Ignorance may be temporary while stupidity can last a lifetime.

- Life, freedom, and independence are profoundly worth defending — but historically, this has always required a superior and well-trained military force.

- A Jew can be stupid, but it is not obligatory. (Simon Wiesenthal).

- Those who cannot remember the past are condemned to repeat it. (George Santayana, 1863-1952).

- Knowledge is power. Knowledge is what makes information valuable. For knowledge to be useful, it must be acted upon.

- Power corrupts, and absolute power corrupts absolutely. (John Emerich Edward Dalberg Acton, 1834—1902).

- All that is necessary for the triumph of evil is that good men do nothing. (Edmund Burke, 1729-1797)

- A government that robs Peter to pay Paul can always depend on the support of Paul. (George Bernard Shaw, 1856-1950).

- We must never take our freedom for granted.

- We must hear the declared as well as the hidden threats of our enemies with the greatest alarm.

- Our wonderful democracy and freedom as we know it today in the United States of America can change, and we must therefore always have vigilance on our side.

- There is a constant need to be fully aware that as long as Jews live in a non-Jewish country, our minority position remains tenuous. History has proven over and over that under any form of government, be it a dictatorship, a monarchy, a democracy, or a benign combination thereof, its citizens can and will turn on its Jewish population on a moment's notice.

The Shoah...

The Shoah has more than adequately proven to those with open eyes and ears that any religious, political, or monetary enticement (or any combination thereof) will cause a large portion of citizens to cause irreparable damage to its Jewish or other minority populations.

✿

Holocaust Timeline:
As experienced
by a survivor from Hungary

1938: HUNGARY PASSES ANTI-SEMITIC LAWS
Horthy Miklós, the ruler of Hungary, agrees to pass a series of anti-Semitic laws. He hopes that by befriending Hitler, Hungary will gain Germany's political support for the return of the territory Hungary lost after World War I, at the Trianon Peace Treaty of 1919/1920.

LATE 1938: HUNGARY GAINS TERRITORY
Shortly thereafter, with the encouragement and blessings of Hitler's Germany, Hungary annexes large sections of Slovakia.

1939: MORE TERRITORY FOR HUNGARY
With the further blessings of Hitler's Germany, Hungary eagerly takes possession of additional hefty portions of the Sub-Carpathian region that were formerly part of Czechoslovakia and Ruthenia (Máramaros).

1939/1940: MORE FROM ROMANIA
With the encouragement of Hitler's Germany, Hungary takes over and annexes Northern Transylvania, from Romania.

1939/1940: IMMENSE PAYBACK TO GERMANY!
Hungary proudly joins the Axis Powers: Germany, Italy and Japan.

DEC. 13, 1940: WAR ON U.S.
Hungary declares war on the United States of America.

1941: WAR ON RUSSIA
Hungary declares war on the Soviet Union, joining Nazi Germany in its loud-mouthed war effort, to destroy and annihilate Russia.

All the above military and political actions in Hungary, as well as its numerous newly-passed anti-Semitic laws, led to a massive loss of Jewish blood, and much Jewish suffering in Hungary and its neighboring countries. The following are some of these edicts:

1. All Jews of Polish or other ethnic origin who resided in Greater Hungary between the years of 1830 to 1942 — whether for a short time or for generations — were required to prove their families' Hungarian citizenship as far back as before 1830. If they could not do so, they were hastily arrested and their entire families were deported to Poland or the Ukraine. The Government permitted them to take along one small personal package per person. Their neighbors, the local municipality and the Hungarian Government promptly appropriated all their possessions and properties. Expediently, the Hungarians cleverly referred to these stolen properties as "abandoned property."

We later learned that the Hungarians, in collaboration with the Polish and Ukrainian Nazis, delivered about one-third of the deportees to the food-deprived and overcrowded Jewish ghettos of Poland or Ukraine. They took another third to the Polish and Ukrainian forests and shot them en masse. The balance was driven fully clothed into raging rivers to drown or burned to death.

2. By the end of the year 1941, a large number of Hungarian Jewish professionals and businesses experienced trouble renewing their annual licenses. The officials in charge shamelessly advised them that if they paid a large amount of cash "under the table," an effort would be made to renew their license. At the same time, if a gentile wanted a license held by a Jew, the Jew's license was promptly revoked and issued to the non-Jewish petitioner.

From this point on, all Hungarian Jews had to prove their indispensability to a particular job or trade. Any Jew unable to provide acceptable proof of this was deprived of his position. This occurred in all public institutions as well as in many private industries. Therewith, Jews became unable to earn a wage to feed their families. Additionally, they became the first to be fired and the last to be hired.

3. The Hungarians readily copied the Germans in their heinous actions against loyal Jewish citizens. We became a defenseless minority whose longstanding citizenship rights quickly disappeared and whose courageous sacrifices in the service of our country before and during World War I were simply nullified. Jews became scapegoats for the slightest imaginable excuse.

4. The systematic spreading of anti-Semitism was sophisticated and unrelenting. Everyone was busy, including legislators in passing anti-Semitic laws, schools in teaching hatred to students, radios were blaring venom and bigotry, and newspapers writing slander. It was a well-prepared plan, and the high doses of anti-Semitism successfully infected the population.

5. Every move we made could be a matter of life or death. The civilian population beat Jews on the streets with impunity. We became the hunted people of Hungary. Our personal property and business possessions made us an inviting and profitable victim to exploit.

6. In order to feed their families, even austerely, Jews of all former professions became street peddlers and beggars. As a direct result, Jewish communal life also suffered. Large numbers of Jews were unable to pay their synagogue dues. The income of most Jewish community organizations' sank to such low levels that the majority of them were unable to retain their employees.

Bergen-Belsen 'via' Numbers

After the British Army liberated the Bergen Belsen district, they found an unbelievable sight of human misery in the huge area of the Bergen Belsen Concentration Camp. The Encyclopedia Britannica states that in Bergen Belsen, "more than 35,000 people died between January and mid-April of 1945... from starvation." Note that these 35,000 victims of German cruelty and brutality died during a short 3.5-month period.

Throughout its years of existence, the Bergen Belsen Concentration Camps saw the willful murder and starvation of approximately an additional 40,000 human victims.

Post WWII reports on Hungarian Jewry

According to reliable reports, the number of Hungarian Jews in 1941 was 725,000, plus 100,000 converts to Christianity. The Hungarian Government identified the converts, too, as Jews,* and all anti-Jewish laws affected them as well, making a total of 825,000 men, women and children who were in danger of annihilation.

---

* Many descendants of Jews who had converted to Christianity were considered Jewish. In addition, the definition of a Jew was stricter in Hungary than in Germany itself: A half-Jew married to a quarter-Jew was considered Jewish in Hungary, but not in Germany.

Conspiring together, the Germans and Hungarians forced all Jews throughout Hungary into Ghettos and then delivered them in locked cattle boxcars to Auschwitz-Birkenau for extermination.

In the spring of 1944, about 7,000 to 10,000 Hungarian Jews arrived each day at Auschwitz-Birkenau. The German SS gassed/choked and burned about 80 to 90% of these unfortunates on the first day of their arrival.* The number of Hungarian Jewish victims of the Holocaust is estimated at 565,000. "Only with the unfettered cooperation and active participation of the Hungarian state could the Germans have succeeded in nearly erasing Hungary's once devoted Jewish population."

In a book entitled *The World Must Know*, published by the U.S. Holocaust Memorial Museum, Michael Berenbaum wrote: "Between May 14 and July 8, 1944, 437,402 Jews from 55 Hungarian localities were deported to Auschwitz in 147 trains. Most were gassed at Birkenau soon after they arrived."

The German SS, with the help of volunteer SS men from Ukraine, Poland, Hungary, Slovakia, etc., continued with the daily extermination of the remainder of their families. Only a small percentage of Jews made it through the terrible first phase of selections by Dr. Josef Mengele and his Nazi helpers. This was the daily German routine for murder in Auschwitz-Birkenau and in the various slave labor, concentration and annihilation camps throughout Germany, Poland, Austria, Czechoslovakia, Ukraine, and Belgium and in German/Hungarian-occupied areas of Russia.

The many sub-concentration camps located within a 50- to 60-kilometer range around Auschwitz-Birkenau produced a massive amount of goods and services for the German armed forces and their civilian populations. However, the main function of the Auschwitz-Birkenau camp was murder — gassing

---

* See *The Nazis' Last Victims*, by Randolph L. Braham with Scott Miller, p. 55: "fewer than 5 percent of these deportees ever returned." and, p. 137: "the murder of 560,000 members of the Jewish community,...."

followed by cremation.

The fanatic evil, demonic and racist teachings of hatred and bigotry were so passionate and so effective that the Germans and Hungarians continued the diabolic murder even after they clearly saw their own imminent destruction by the victorious American, Soviet and other Allied soldiers.

A frightening concluding thought

The atrocious exploits of Hitler and his Axis partners led to the deaths of 55 to 60 million people, and about three times as many injured and crippled human beings.

Furthermore, they caused heretofore unimaginable human misery to 200 million people and hundreds of billions in financial losses in term of 1945 dollars.

World War II timetable and notes

NOV. 9, 1938
Kristallnacht: The Nazi German Government coordinates mass civilian and police attacks on Jews, Jewish places of worship, Jewish homes and businesses for the purpose of promoting and encouraging anti-Semitism, prejudice, hatred, and to present opportunities to kill, loot and burn Jews, destroy their homes, demolish and steal their properties.

SEPT. 1, 1939
Germany attacks Poland setting off Hitler's six-year World War II.

JAN. 27, 1945
The Russian Army liberates Auschwitz-Birkenau.

MAY 8, 1945
World War II officially ends in Europe; the Germans, Hungarians, and their European Axis Allies are defeated and unconditionally surrender to the victorious American, Russian and British armies. The world names this event "VE Day 1945, "Victory in Europe Day.

SEPT. 2, 1945
World War II officially ends. Japan surrenders to General of the U.S. Army, General Douglas MacArthur. The Supreme Allied Commander accepts the surrender on board the USS Missouri in Tokyo Bay.

1944-1945 A.Z. timeline:

APRIL 16, 1944

Town Crier announces our expulsion order from Hungary.

APRIL 17, 1944

We are forced into the Brown Layos Castle; the first action in our deportation from our country, Hungary.

APRIL 17/18 TO MAY 21/22, 1944

Our incarceration in the Ghetto of Beregszász.

MAY 21/22 1944

Hungarian gendarmes force us into waiting cattle boxcar trains. There were reportedly four cattle boxcar train transports from the Ghetto of Beregszász to Auschwitz-Birkenau.

MAY 25, THE 3RD DAY OF SIVAN, 1944

We arrive in Auschwitz-Birkenau. My father and brother Sholem Yosef are murdered on the day of arrival.

JUNE 14, 1944, THE 23RD DAY OF SIVAN

My Mommy and sister Gizi are murdered on this day.

JANUARY 11, 1945

My last day of work in the Jaworzno coal mines.
I am admitted into the infirmary.

JANUARY 17, 1945

The Jaworzno Concentration Camp starts the "Death March" from Camp Jaworzno towards Germany, to get away from the advancing Russian Army.

JANUARY 25/26, 1945

Jaworzno is liberated by the advancing Russian Army.

FEBRUARY 2, 1945

I start to walk from Jaworzno to Krakow, Poland.

With the help of a Russian tank-truck, I arrive in Krakow.

FEBRUARY 5, 1945
I leave Krakow to walk to Tarnow.

FEBRUARY 28, 1945
I arrive in Vásárosnamény after being on the road for 24 days.

MAY 8, 1945
VE Day: Germany surrenders; WWII ends in Europe.

MAY ?, 1945
Yahrtzeit of Bina Rivka who died of typhoid fever in Bergen-Belsen during the early days of the British liberation of the death camp.

MAY ?, 1945
Yahrtzeit of Baruch. He died in the Mauthausen Concentration Camp in southern Germany subsequent to his Death March from Auschwitz-Birkenau.

SEPTEMBER 2, 1945
Japan surrenders and World War II officially ends.

Acknowledgements

From the first time we met until today, I have much admired Dr. Leatrice Rabinsky. She has been a source of continued inspiration to multitudes of students, friends and family. She thoroughly understood the Holocaust survivors' painful reluctance to report their horrific experiences, yet she gently encouraged us to open up and inform the world of our stories.

Yes, it was a painful and most difficult start, but she knew well that if we didn't get over our reluctance, the Holocaust history would die with us and the world would never know. I am forever grateful for her generous advice and long-range vision which raised my spirits and that of many others. May she be blessed with a long and healthy life and may G-d grant her much delight from her wonderful family.

I also wish to express my deepest appreciation and gratitude for their keen insight and diligent guidance during the revision of the manuscript to: Marty Neiditz, Emanuel Weinberger, William Marocco, OBM, Sol Factor, and Leeba Schneck.